Faith for Personal Crises

FAITH
FOR PERSONAL CRISES

By Carl Michalson

CHARLES SCRIBNER'S SONS NEW YORK

PRINTED IN THE UNITED STATES OF AMERICA

LIBRARY OF CONGRESS CATALOG CARD NUMBER 58-5720

ACKNOWLEDGMENTS

I would like to express my appreciation to the following publishers for granting permission for the use of material published by them:

Harcourt, Brace and Company, New York, and Faber and Faber, Ltd., London, for the use of material from T. S. Eliot's THE COCKTAIL PARTY.

The New York Times for material from a commentary by Maurice Valency on the play "Ondine," which appeared on February 14, 1954.

Harper & Brothers, New York, for the use of material from LABOR'S RELATION TO THE CHURCH AND COMMUNITY, edited by Liston Pope.

Abingdon Press, Nashville, Tennessee, for material from THE CREATOR AND THE ADVERSARY by Edwin Lewis.

W. W. Norton & Company, New York, for material from THE NOTES OF MALTE LAURIDS BRIGGE by Rainer Maria Rilke.

The Viking Press, Inc., New York, for material from THE LIVING ROOM by Graham Greene.

Farrar, Straus and Cudahy, Inc., New York, for material from THE DESCENT OF THE DOVE by Charles Williams.

Random House, Inc., New York, and Faber and Faber, Ltd., London, for material from THE AGE OF ANXIETY by W. H. Auden. Copyright 1946, 1947 by W. H. Auden. Reprinted by permission of Random House, Inc.

The Biblical quotations are for the most part from the Revised Standard Version of the Bible, copyrighted 1946 and 1952 by the Division of Christian Education of the National Council of the Churches of Christ in the United States of America.

C. M.

TO JANET
sine qua non

PREFACE

The materials embodied in this book have been developing for quite a long time through my engagements with theological students, pastors, laymen, and college groups. "Going too long," said Jonathan Swift in *Tale of a Tub,* "is a cause of abortion as effectual though not so frequent as going too short, and holds true especially in the labours of the brain." Whether this effort was well conceived and delivered is obviously my responsibility. That it appears at this particular time is the responsibility of President William C. Finch of Southwestern University, Georgetown, Texas. His invitation to give the Willson Lectures in 1957 has occasioned the birth. Five of the chapters of this volume comprised that lectureship.

Among the many others I should thank without implicating is Newman S. Cryer, Jr. He first detected the fetal heartbeat in these materials when he was editor of *The Pastor.* Mrs. Pat Winters typed the manuscript and helped with the proofs.

C. M.

DREW FOREST
MADISON, N. J.

CONTENTS

ONE

A Theology for Crucial Situations

"These clever men are all so stupid; there's no one for me to talk to . . . always alone, alone, I haven't a soul . . . and who I am, and why I am, nobody knows."

—CHARLOTTA IN CHEKHOV'S *The Cherry Orchard*

"I want to help you. I want to be of use. I would want it if it were the last thing in life I could have. But when I talk, my tongue is heavy with the . . . Catechism."

—FATHER JAMES IN GRAHAM GREENE'S *The Living Room*

Theology in recent years has been learning to speak a new language. The lofty, high-pitched tone which characterized its speech when it was queen of all the sciences has given way to *sotto voce*. This turn of events was first anticipated by Jesus who said, "Whoever would be great among you must be your servant, . . . even as the Son of man came not to be served but to serve." Impetus was surely given to the trend the day St. Francis of Assisi stopped the discourse of a theologian to allow Brother Giles to speak. Most recently, with the rise of psychotherapy people inside and outside the church have turned for the care of their souls to the nontheological sciences. The pastors of churches, still the most overworked personal counselors in society today, have found themselves confronted with questions for which they recognize no answers from within their bulk of professional information. Anxious to be helpful, they have therefore turned for sources of help to the anthropological sciences most immediately taken up with the problems of the people. In the process, they have extended the short arm of professional therapy in a way miraculously beneficial to the public health.

The question which the reformers of the sixteenth century raised concerning the proper care of souls, however, stands over the situation in the church today. Is not the shepherd of souls "one who makes the deed of Christ effective," one who helps his brother the better to know and to do God's will? That is the way Martin Bucer asked the question in his treatise on *The True Care of Souls and the Right Kind of Shepherding*. Is not the sign of a true shepherd that he "lead his sheep in no other way than that in which *he* is led, in the knowledge and trust of God?" Huldreich Zwingli raised the question in that way in his treatise, *Der Hirt, The Shepherd*. Is not the ministry of the church responsible to its craft only when it addresses the needs of the people from the deepest resources available in the Christian faith?

A similar judgment stands over the work of theology in the church today. The result is that theology has entered into a period of exhilaration unparalleled since the Reformation. A theologian who does not think of the Christian faith in relation to the needs of the people has defaulted in his responsibility to the practicing church. Moreover, he has missed the joy of theology, and to miss the joy is to miss all. For when the faith of the church is held in responsibility to the lives of the people, two startling phenomena occur. In the first place, one sees meanings in the faith itself which might otherwise have gone quite unnoticed. In the second place, one experiences the sense of satisfaction that comes with being relevant in some direct though modest way.

This series of studies is an attempt to enter into the current theological opportunity. Even though it does not speak with the stentorian accents of a theology of more regal days, possibly its whispers will be heard. They are directed to the tenderest and most sensitive needs in the human spirit, the crucial situations in the lives of the people.

A "crucial situation" is a highly specialized kind of situation profoundly suited to theological concern. To do justice to its meaning, three levels of definition are needed. First of all, *a crucial situation is an inescapable situation, requiring decisiveness.* It is not just any old situation. It is a situation in which one exists of necessity, just by virtue of being a person. It is a situation in which there is no neutrality. The taking of an attitude and the making of a decision is inseparable from the situation. There is in it what the gestalt psychologist Wolfgang Koehler called the "aha!" ingredient. Crucial situations offer the possibility of being surprised in such a way as to feel one's own selfhood more intensely and the possibility of being called to assume responsibility for oneself more resolutely.

Elton Trueblood's little book, *Common Ventures,** deals with four such situations: birth, marriage, work, and death. That no one can escape birth and death goes without saying. But the inescapable element which makes them crucial is not their brute factuality. It is the element which makes decision unavoidable. One must take an attitude toward his birth and his death. These situations are critical, because one's entire demeanor between these two events

* The first in the series of Willson Lectures at Southwestern University.

hinges upon the decision he makes concerning them. The issue of birth and death is the issue of origin and destiny. On the back of that definition work and marriage ride in as inescapable situations. One may be a tramp or a bachelor, but he cannot escape the crisis of vocation and marriage, for inseparable from being a person is the "live option" of working and marrying.

Soren Kierkegaard is the author of a series of three religious discourses entitled *Thoughts on Crucial Situations in Life*. One discourse is designed to be heard on the occasion of a marriage, another on the occasion of a funeral, and the third prior to making one's confession. One must decide what attitude he will take toward his guilt or sense of unworthiness, just as truly as toward the possibility of death and marriage. Karl Jaspers, the contemporary German philosopher, re-enforces and extends this list. He calls them "limit-situations" or "boundary-situations." It is within these experiences that the person "comes up against it" in life. In the process he finds something out about his possibilities and about his needs. There is the situation of death, of guilt, of the struggle for power which one associates with the vocational life, and of the struggle for love which one associates with marriage. There is also the situation of suffering. Buffeting against these limits, the self begins to find itself in the fashion of a mountain stream which bounces off this rock and that, until its course has been defined. In his *Courage to Be* Paul Tillich adds another crucial situation. To the situations of guilt and death, which are confrontations with condemnation and finitude, he adds the situation of doubt, which is the threat of meaninglessness. To be a person is to face the question as to whether life is significant. That question places one in the crucial situation of doubt.

All seven of these crucial situations will be entered into here. In each case there will be an effort to determine what makes them crucial and what the Christian faith has to offer as guidance to a person living through the situation. Guilt, doubt, vocation, marriage, suffering and death will be dealt with in that order. Basic to all the situations, and the ingredient most likely to contribute to crisis is anxiety. Anxiety is really the primal situation. It results from an inadequate handling of the question of one's very identity, the attitude one holds toward one's very birth. Hence, a consideration of anxiety will lead the list.

The second factor that makes these situations crucial is that they are *situations in which it is being determined whether one will live or die.* This is probably the most literal meaning of the word "crisis." A crisis in an illness is that point where it is being determined whether the patient will survive. In a business it is that stage at which the solvency of the enterprise is at stake, or in an historical movement where the water-shed between rise and decline is traversed. In these situations one is faced, then, not simply with live options but with what William James called "forced" options. If one does not go forward, he will go backward. If one does not succeed, he will fail. It is parallel to the navigation of a sailboat. As Kierkegaard has said, one must know when to "come about," or he will run aground. The rower at a certain point on a swift river must decide to which shore he will pull, or the rapids will decide for him! The kingdom of God comes in such a way. It is the *kairos,* the right time. In that time, "he that is not for me is against me," said Jesus. Crucial situations are

like the kingdom of God. R.S.V.P. is written over each
of them. Response is required. Not to act in itself constitutes refusal. Why these particular situations exemplify
this meaning of a crisis can best be illustrated when the
crises themselves are discussed.

The third factor which makes a situation crucial is that
there is in it a dimension of ultimate significance. Not
just metaphorically but actually the question of the kingdom of God is involved. In every human crisis there is a
God-relation. This makes the option not simply "live"
and "forced" but "momentous" as well. The "live" and
"forced" elements in the situations are what arouse the
concerns and deplete the energies of people, and, making
them wretched, prompt them to seek help. The "momentous" element is the Christian faith's authentic channel
of access to the people in these situations. Without this
dimension, a theology for crucial situations could legitimately be accused of gathering apologetic figs from pathological thistles, exploiting the weaknesses of people in
order to strengthen the influence of the church.

The English word *crisis* is cognate with the Greek word
krisis. Whenever this word appears in the New Testament
it has a single meaning, "judgment." As I have said, in
every crucial situation a judgment, a decision is required.
But in the New Testament, the judgment referred to is
never simply the judgment man must make. It is always
the judgment God has made. No discussion of crucial
situations in life would satisfy the New Testament understanding of life which did not see within the situation the
imminence of the Judgment of God, which is the presence
of God's decision upon human life. No crucial situation
is adequately lived through, therefore, which does not take

into consideration the dimension of the God-relation. "What does God intend?" "What, therefore, must I do?" These two questions interpenetrate in every crucial situation.

Theology has a standard way of saying this: man is made in the image of God. Therefore, nothing that man does is a fully human act which does not take God into consideration. Now, what it means to say of man that he is made in the image of God has become highly ambiguous, considering modern man's lively metaphorical sense. The Christian doctrine of man as image of God, however, does not draw upon the metaphor from the plastic arts. Theology does not mean that God has made man as a miniature model of Himself. Were God to have done this, He would have violated one of His own commands and tempted man to do the same: "thou shalt not make any graven image!" Nor does Christian doctrine draw upon the metaphor from genealogy. You can say of the natural son of your friend, "He's the spitting image of his father." But you cannot say that of man's relation to God. For God has no blood relatives, no genealogical descendants, save His "only-begotten Son." Man is not a child of God; he is a creature of God. If he is a child in any sense, it is not by natural descent but only by adoption. I do not say this to down-grade man. Anyone who suspects so does not appreciate what really happens in the adoption of children. I know of one childless couple who adopted a little girl. As often happens, thereafter a child was born to them. The little adopted child felt so sorry for the new baby brother that she insisted her parents take out adoption papers for him. In the same way, a man can be overcome with the sense of gratitude at being God's adopted child.

The metaphor invoked by the doctrine of the image of God is taken neither from the plastic arts nor from genealogy. It is a relational metaphor. Man is a being created with the responsibility for reflecting the reality of God as in a mirror. By this is not meant that somehow on the face of his life man must develop a resemblance to God. That would be to revert to the inferences in the genealogical metaphor. It means that man's life takes on a posture defined by the open acknowledgment that there is a God, and a demeanor consistent with the knowledge of who God is. The Christian man's responsibility is not to become like God, so that people will preoccupy themselves with contemplating God's image upon the Christian's face. The Christian man holds his life in relation to God in such a way that others are influenced to see what he sees and to posture their lives in the same direction. "To be *like* God" is not man's responsibility; it is his sin. By that temptation the serpent originally sets man against his creator. (Gen. 3:5) To be *responsible* to God is man's task, and that task defines his very being as a man.

This is really why the Epistle of James in the New Testament calls God a "jealous God." If you, for instance, were to take your wife to a party, but from the moment you entered the door she were to leave your arm and reflect the existence of every other man at that party but you, you would be jealous. You would almost have a right to be. Well, God has made man a being who is responsible for reflecting His reality. When man goes around reflecting the existence of every other kind of reality but God, God is jealous, and He has a right to be.

Many do not wish to refer to God as jealous, on the grounds that one ought not attribute to God characteristics which one would not care to see in one's friends. Two things should be said of that complaint, just to keep the record straight. In the first place, jealousy is inappropriate to our friends just because it is so exclusively appropriate to God. There is no other reality of whom it can be said that he deserves our complete attention. Therefore there is no other reality but God which has any innate right to jealousy when that attention is not given. In the second place, I use the word "jealousy" here not in its popular, emotional sense, but in its preferred dictionary definition: "exacting exclusive devotion; intolerant of rivalry." In that case, God cannot help being jealous. It is not an emotional reaction. It is His business as God. It is not a characteristic; it is a responsibility.

One day at luncheon with my family, remembering an article my wife had recently read me on how parents should make edifying conversation with their children, I turned to my son and asked, "Steve, what's your philosophy of life?" Immediately he replied, "We're talking bears!" It seems they had just been reading the story of the three bears in school, and the teacher explained to the children that bears don't really talk. Men are the only talking animals. What my son meant to say, therefore, was that man is a talking animal.

This, I believe, is an improvement upon Plato's definition of man as a "featherless biped." But Aristotle had already made the improvement by calling man "a rational animal." In the intervening years, man has been called "a tool-making animal," and various other sorts of animal. But I found my son's definition as good as any, and suggested a revision at precisely the same point at which I would wish to revise these other definitions of man. Man

is not to be defined in terms of his relationship to the
animal world, but in terms of his relationship to *God*. If
he must be called a talking animal, then the characteristic
thing about him is not his capacity for rational speech but
his ability to talk in a very special way: to project his
speech beyond himself in the direction of the hidden
reality called "God." Man is a *praying* animal.

That, then, is the meaning of the crucial situations
which this series of studies will undertake to examine. If
a crisis is, as I have said, a situation which everyone is
undergoing just by virtue of being human, then you can
see how very relevant it is for the Christian faith to speak
to men through the medium of these situations. Conversa-
tions often lag between people. One scarcely dares to
answer some people's questions, as Jean-Paul Sartre has
said, because the moment you commence talking, they begin to yawn. The best way to guarantee an attentive
audience would be to address them at some one of these
points of universal concern. The key to the most effective
communication in any area of life will probably be found
to lie in the use of these very situations as points of con-
tact.

The genius of the situations, however, is that while
they pertain to everyone, they do not pertain to everyone
in the same way. Each must decide for himself about his
situation. Hence the universality of the situations is over-
laid with an exceeding individuality. Death, which happens to everyone, suggests *my* death. Work, guilt, and the
other situations in which all men live engulf me as an
individual and elicit my personal concern.

Theology knows something about every individual in
each situation, however, that the man may not know about

himself. Yet this knowledge is the clue to an adequate negotiation of the situation. Man is made to image God, and if he is not doing this, he is defaulting in his responsibility as a man and jarring the conditions upon which life may be well led. A theology which is sensitive to the crucial situations of life will have as its mission the mobilizing of those affirmations in the Christian faith which shed the most light upon the meaning of man's life before God in these crises.

Now theology is the intellectual elucidation of the Christian faith. Theology is the process of patterning the mind with the logic of the Christian belief, to the end that the communication of that belief to oneself or to others may have the maximum chance of being intelligible. If one does not have a theologically patterned mind, when he speaks he will do nothing but confuse. He might better remain silent. But even silence, which does not presuppose a patterned mind, can be confusing. A young man and young woman may be sitting together on a sofa. There may be utter silence between them. If he has no pattern on his mind, the situation can be oppressively dull. If he has a patterned mind, notwithstanding the silence, the moment can be electrically significant. The same is true of the ministry of silence in crucial situations. In the crisis of death, for instance, one may minister in silence. But there can be two kinds of silence. One may communicate nothing but stupefaction about the meaning of death, in which case there is no ministry at all. Another may through his theologically well-patterned silence fill the air with the assurance that "the Lord is my shepherd, I shall not want." The aim of a theology for crucial situations is to pattern the mind with the resources in the Christian faith for meeting personal crises.

In order to concede that this *is* theology, one must be aware that there is more than one way of doing theology. There are several more traditional forms of theology. Biblical theology organizes the insights of the Bible in terms of the language of the Bible. Historical theology organizes the insights of the Christian church around dominant motifs in the history of the faith. Dogmatic theology organizes the faith in terms of the interior coherence of the faith as it is seen in each successive generation in the light of developing Biblical and historical understanding.

Alongside these more traditional forms of theology is what might be called a cultural theology, which organizes the meaning of the Christian faith around motifs which become dominant in the spirit of any given age. This is what Paul Tillich has called "an honest theology of cultural high standing" or what Schleiermacher directed to "the cultured among the despisers of religion." It is peculiarly fitted to win credence for the Christian faith from the more sophisticated sectors of society.

There is also, however, what has classically been called a practical theology. Here the insights of the faith are assembled around the needs of the operating church. It is a kind of functional or operational theology. There is a theology for worship, a liturgical theology. There is a theology for religious education, a catechetical theology. There is a theology for preaching, a homiletical theology. There is a theology for church unity, an ecumenical theology.

The theology that is being done in this volume is, I believe, what might be called a poimenical theology, a theology for the proper shepherding of sheep. (The Greek word, *poimen,* is the word for shepherd.) Restricting the scope of the treatment to the personal crises in the lives of the people, it is simply one branch of the care of souls. I have called that branch a theology for crucial situations. Unlike the traditional forms of theology, such as Biblical, historical, and dogmatic theology, it does not need to say everything there is to say about the faith. It says only what is immediately pertinent to the situations at hand. It may even deliberately soft-pedal some elements in the total body of belief which might obstruct the healing process. It has the aim of relieving rather than intensifying the crisis. It will not deal in magnitudes of knowledge, for what is needed in a crucial situation is not true propositions but an understanding of one's life. Nor will it become authoritarian and directive, insisting on the truth of its claims. There is just no point in that. Under conditions of crisis the truth must validate itself, entering as a liberating perspective. There is only one test of truth within a crucial situation: Does it illuminate and heal? Even that test cannot be applied before the therapeutic process has set in.

Here, then, begins a theology for crucial situations. What *has* the Christian faith to say when the obstetric force of personal crises draws it out at its points of greatest relevance?

TWO

The Crisis of Anxiety

"We discover that we do not know our role; we look for a
mirror; we want to remove our make-up and take off what is
false and be real. But somewhere a piece of disguise that we
forgot still sticks to us. A trace of exaggeration remains in our
eyebrows; we do not notice that the corners of our mouth are
bent. And so we walk around, a mockery and a mere half;
neither having achieved being nor actors."

—RAINER MARIA RILKE, *The Notes of Malte Laurids Brigge*.

"Anxiety arises from one's comparing himself with others. He
should only compare himself with Christ."

—BLAISE PASCAL, *Pensées*.

Nothing significant would ever be accomplished without the aid of anxiety. This ought to be acknowledged clearly lest the filter of therapy be expected
to strain all the stimulants from the smoke of anxiety. For
anxiety is an emotional exhilaration. It rewards us for
our perilously elevated hopes. Students who aim high
academically will be anxious. Parents who share the aim
also will be anxious. But the sheer stimulation of the
anxiety is part of the incentive for the undertaking. The
boy who makes love will be anxious. The girl who is
loved will also be anxious. Blushing, palpitation, light-
headedness, and the exquisitely painful sensation of love
are panic symptoms and hence the signs of anxiety. But
they are also the very gratifications which continue to draw

14

people together. Graduates who choose vocations consistent with high concepts of themselves will be anxious. But the anxiety does for the long haul through college and graduate school what caffein does for the night before exams. It painlessly flagellates an otherwise flagging spirit and promotes conditions favorable to carrying out mature commitments.

Anxiety is the exhilarating emotional response to danger. Every sort of high resolve forces that response upon us. Stretched between what one believes he should become and what one really is, one undergoes a tension in life analogous to the panic thrill of descent. Probably no one would ride roller coasters were it not for the threat of descent, which is the thrill. Some would seldom kiss without the thrill of the blush which is the fear of being "let down." Likewise to choose high aims in life is to court the panic in the fear of failure and rejection. In small doses it can produce the vigilance whereby achievement is attained. It is no accident, then, that great achievement has been accounted for since Plato as "the gift of madness," an ancient name for anxiety.

Anxiety is not always exhilarating, however. It can also be depressing. For some, anxiety is a spur at the flank of life. It keeps us on the move. It is a tickle and titillation in the spirit. For others, it is a thorn in the flesh, a stimulation so excessive that it irritates, wounds, and finally breaks us. Anxiety is a poison. Depending on the proportions, it can be either curative or sickening. Building up in our spirit it can make us giddy and gay. When it swells unmanageably, however, it can rupture and spread through the whole system of our life, tincturing and torturing the tissue of every relationship. It is because anxiety can be such basic evil that the liberation of man will not come without attention to it.

A young woman sits down to write a letter. She is intent upon breaking her engagement. But her hand cramps stiff with paralysis. That paralysis is a form of hysteria which expresses acute anxiety and disrupts the normal stream of life. Or a young man sits down to study for exams. His mind goes blank. It remains blank for days to come, beyond even the day of exams. Or, a man appears before a prospective employer to advance his credentials for a position. His mouth dries up so that his tongue sticks and he is engulfed by taciturnity. All such calamities are associated in some way with anxiety. If all anxiety were only exhilarating, we could revel in it. Since some anxiety is depressing, it is not altogether innocent. It should be isolated, identified, and subjected to analysis, which is the psychological preface to liberation.

The revealing thing about depressive emotional reactions is that they are usually out of proportion to the apparent dangers. A mother who observes a wart on the hand of her child has a right to be anxious. Public information about cancer has alerted us to apparently innocent skin blights, arousing enough anxiety to motivate early care and treatment. When the mother confronted by a wart screams and stiffens in hysteria, one gets the impression that her reaction is somewhat disproportionate to the clear danger. A hunter facing a lion in the African jungles with his gun jammed has a right to be anxious. But if a grown man retreats in dread at the sight of a common cat, something is clearly wrong. His anxiety makes no sense. It is unrelated to any known danger of sufficient grimness to account for his panic reaction. In the same way, letter-writing cannot explain the correspondent's hand. Academic exercises ought not immobilize the student's brain. Employers do not normally shock one speechless.

Anxiety, therefore, is not fully defined until it is related to some hidden danger sufficient to account for extreme reactions. The blemish on the hand of the child may be seen as a wart by the mother—even a cancerous wart; but it may also be seen as a syphilitic sore. She had always been threatened by the judgment that sex relations outside of marriage are punishable by venereal diseases transmissible to offspring. Now, she had never had sex relations outside of marriage, but she had always wanted to. In this moment, therefore, her sense of guilt was being projected into the wart on her daughter's hand. The wart in itself is inadequate to account for the panic reactions. Some such hidden danger as an unconscious sense of guilt makes the hysteria plausible.

Paralysis in many of its forms results when objective desires are disrupted by subjective or hidden fears. Much loss of memory is the result of the collision between the desire to concentrate and the secret fear of the outcome. The inner voice—real but unheard: ("I could become a skillful surgeon; but then I would be disappointing my father who wants me to continue his legal practice!"). Taciturnity, which like forgetfulness may be a form of hysterical paralysis, is the short-circuiting of a concrete desire by an invisible fear, immobilizing the speaker. The inner voice, again: ("I want this job, but it will make me independent of my parents whose happiness depends so largely on my needing them!"). Such deeply inward alternatives leave one as rigid as the proverbial donkey between equidistant haystacks. These are the paralyses that will never be cured by medication or massage, for their source is hidden deep within the spirit of the man where manual therapy is futile.

Now, few people are actually paralyzed by anxiety. But almost everyone is a little stiffened by it. There is what Sigmund Freud has called "the psychopathology of everyday life" which expresses itself in only mild frustrations. These blocks are not big enough to break us, but they do fracture our lives. They continuously cripple our capacity for creativity and repeatedly retard our relationships with others. Among them can be numbered such otherwise explicable and innocent phenomena as fatigue and drowsiness, excitability and aggressiveness, and the gnawing option in our life between the passion for flight and the passion to fight.

These minor cracks in our life can be easily papered over by daily effort. They begin to show up, however, in crucial situations. Unseaworthy ships are not exposed by calm seas and harbors. Almost imperceptible splits in major political parties only come to the fore when political activities are intensified. In the same way, tiny emotional fissures can become gaping wounds. It is when the spirit is jarred by crises, that the soul is "cracked across by care." (Baudelaire)

For this reason anxiety is so basic an ingredient in every crisis experience. A life that is meant to perform as a whole is constantly being placed in situations which demand wholeness. Anxiety, however, cripples the life inwardly, breaking it in two by what the psychologists call the ambivalence of fear and desire. Theologians call it the two laws warring in our members. It is the collision of normal desires with insurmountable expectations and fears. Consider the strains which the mature demands of life put upon a person. If he is in school, he must put his whole attention upon his work. If he is not whole, how will he meet the demands of formal education without simply illustrating his brokenness? Every able-bodied person is expected to respond to the demands of vocation. Now a vocation demands a person's entire life, but if he is not whole, what else can the "work-load" do but provide the occasion for a breakdown. Again, it is the normal expectation of our culture that a person will marry. Marriage calls upon a person to give himself wholly to another person. If one is not whole, the demands of marriage will simply provide the extra shock that breaks him along the lines of his inner division. Formal education, marriage, and vocation are some of the situations in life most likely to produce breakdown, simply because they are the situations most requiring wholeness.

A man can be broken in two with his inner conflicts. A man whose conscious desires are thwarted by his unconscious fears is a dis-solute man. Required to be one, to be single, to be whole (*solus*), he lives in constant peril of dis-solution by anxiety. The situations of life which exact decisiveness and resolution cannot be wholesomely met by men who are fatiguing themselves inwardly by unresolved tensions. Implosion (a word atomic physics gives us) is the inward chafing of the personality by virtue of its own disunity. Implosion precedes and sets off the explosion of the personality. Because one implodes before he explodes, there is no real therapy in simply binding up the loose pieces of the personality or in cushioning society against the shock of explosive people. This is why faith is relevant to crisis. For faith unifies one's life interiorly. Hence faith directs itself to the ingredient in life most provocative of crisis, namely, anxiety. Anxiety is the result of not knowing who you really are and to whom you really belong. Faith is primarily man's access to an understanding of himself and his obligations. When one knows who he really is, and what therefore he must do, the factors which produce anxiety are reduced, and a man is given access to a life of wholeness and health. In this way faith makes the dis-solute life resolute. How and why that is so remains the burden of this series of studies.

A man must find out who he is. This is not an option; it is a requirement in our very existence as men. Animals cannot; they are too opaque in the blindness of their instincts. Angels need not; they are transparent in their relation to God. Man alone is the being who must reach out in quest of his identity. A man is wrong, therefore, to think of himself as a privileged being. Man is a being constituted solely by responsibility, namely, the responsibility to choose for himself who he is and to pursue that choice responsibly. Man *is* the risk in this decision; he is the project in which the decision continually results. By virtue of this risk he can sink deeper in the scale of being than animals, if misery and degeneracy are any criteria. But for the same reason, he can rise higher in the scale of being than angels, if contentment and creativity are any criteria.

When the Danish playwright, Holberg, wrote his comedy about the peasant Jeppe, he told the story of man's basic quest. For man is a being who comes to consciousness in a world which does not explain him. Hence Jeppe, when he awakens from a drunk in the bed of the Prince of Denmark, the butt of a practical joke, can only ask, "Where is Jeppe?" Who man is cannot be defined, however, by simple location. Man seems thrown into the world like a marble into mud. Somehow he is stuck fast here, but there is nothing in his surroundings that explains him. There is, however, a centrifugal force, a homesickness in his life which keeps the question of his identity alive. Man comes to birth in the world, as Jean-Paul Sartre says, as a man awakens in his bed, clinging to its sides from a dream he had. He will not be satisfied with his life here until he knows what it is that makes him hold on so.

Failure to understand oneself is not as innocent as other kinds of ignorance. Ignorance in general can be absorbed by good humor and the will to live. But ignorance of who one is muddies the waters at their source and the navigation of life can only be a kind of panic vagrancy. One who does not know himself is affected by crucial situations, as Kierkegaard has said, in the same way as storms at sea affect the pilot who thought he knew everything about sailing. Crises expose us as hurricanes break in upon the orderly arrangements of one's privacy. (Joseph Conrad)

Not to know who we are and why we are here and what we ought to be doing is the source of the major mechanism by which we prepare for our anxieties. Not knowing who we are, we invent an understanding of ourselves by which to try to live. Ignorance then gives way to mendacity. Like the proverbial "cat on a hot tin roof," we find our disguise untenable and leap into an identity of our own fabrication. For want of knowledge about ourselves we substitute a lie. (Romans 1:25) In this way man's life is a floating on the vast and uncertain sea of the lie, mid-way between the ignorance in which we are conceived and the knowledge which alone redeems us.

The lie about ourselves gives rise to two types of personalities. One is the type who sets up an image of himself and identifies himself with that image. The other is the type who projects an image of what he feels he ought to be and then sentences his life to the long process of attempting to achieve the image. The former may be called the rebellious type. He revolts against any insinuation that he is not fully coexistent with his image. His rebellion makes him a master at deception, for he must hide any traces of failure to be what he thinks he is. The other may be called the recessive type. His projected image seems so exalted to him that the thought of achieving it fatigues him. Hence, he becomes a master at rationalization, making excuses for his failures even in advance of trying to achieve.

A third type of personality emerges out of sheer dissatisfaction with the other two, yet with no better alternative to pursue. This type is called the resigned type, refusing to camouflage as the rebellious, and refusing to rationalize as the recessive. He simply yields to his inability to establish his identity successfully.

Now one might tend to reject these personality types on the ground that they are too clinical. They are apt to appear only in psychiatric wards or in the waiting rooms of psychoanalysts. It is true that they correspond directly to the account of neurotic mechanisms given in the writings of the psychoanalyst Karen Horney. She labels the mechanisms "the expansive," "the self-effacing," and "the resigned." That is why it is all the more impressive to see how familiar these types can seem when illustrations are taken, as will be done here, from the non-clinical data of everyday life. It is almost startling, for instance, to see three characters in W. H. Auden's *Age of Anxiety* described in terms illustrative of these types before us here.

> Emble says, "How nice it feels
>   To be out ahead." [That will be the monomania of the rebellious type.]
> And Rosetta:
>   ". . . I can't hope to be first
>   So let me be last." [The recessive are easily recognizable by that sentiment.]
> And Quant:
>   "The safest place
>   Is the more or less middling: the mean average
>   Is not noticed." [This does not quite do justice to the resigned mechanism, but comes close.]

One of my friends has aptly summarized these human approaches to life as the mechanisms of "shine," "whine," and "repine."

Why are these mechanisms called anxiety types? Because they build their lives on ignorance of the most important thing to know, and in the process they move against the basic condition of reality. This is the almost proverbial rubbing of the fur of life the wrong way, or moving against the grain of the universe. As Martin Luther once suggested, the heart empty of self-knowledge is not sheer static hollowness. It is emptiness in motion. It is like a millstone, constantly grinding. If there be no wheat of self-knowledge, the heart grinds itself away. Augustine said the same thing but with a different metaphor: "Thou wilt be broken if thou fallest out of thy maker's hands."

These three personality types may seem a bit academic and schematic. The best way to appreciate them is to see them in the context of real life situations. Conversely, the best way to appreciate the dynamics of life situations is to realize that such personality formations are being insinuated into one's adjustment to life and to our detriment. Both devices will be pursued in this series of discussions. The subsequent chapters in the series will deal with the situations of life which are most crucial: guilt, doubt, vocation, marriage, suffering, and death. These are crucial situations because they are the situations that require resoluteness of persons. The inability to resolve oneself in the face of these demands illustrates the dissolution of the self and precipitates the panic symptoms of anxiety. How this is so, and how faith can reduce the anxiety in these situations will be the main task of each of the following discussions. For anxiety is not itself a crucial situation. It is rather the emotional ingredient in all situations which makes them crucial.

The personality types themselves are best understood, however, when they are seen not so much in relation to crises as in relation to the more general anxiety-producing situations of life. There are three such situations. To begin with, let me briefly outline them. First, there is what might be called the *cosmic* situation. It is the situation of life in the cosmos, the world. The very situation elicits the expectation of welfare and security, the maintaining of a livelihood. When the fear that the world will not support us collides with the desire for that support, anxiety formations begin.

Second, there is the *social* situation. This situation is defined by the legitimate expectation for status among one's fellows. This desire is indicated in the very structure of social life. But when this desire is in conflict with the fear that such acceptance is not forthcoming, a turbulent emotion begins to brew within us resulting in personality formations of a very characteristic sort.

Third, there is what might be called the *ontic* situation, to draw on the Greek word meaning "being." The ontic situation is the least apparent and the most significant dimension of human life. Here the question of our very life, our very being, is at stake: its meaning, its freedom from condemnation, and its ultimate continuity. This is life not simply at the level of *bios*, the Greek word from which we get our word "biology." It is the kind of life which the New Testament calls *Zoe*, for which the descriptive adjective is usually "abundant." Here doubt threatens meaning, guilt threatens our justifiability, and death threatens our eternal hopes. When the expectations in our very being are cut across by these poignant threats, anxieties which are least amenable to scrutiny develop, and at levels most profoundly disturbing to the whole of life.

The question before us is this: how does the human personality adapt itself to these anxiety-producing situations? How do the three personality types manifest themselves in their accommodation to these situations? The answer to this question at this juncture would seem fantastic unless it is already known what an enormous capacity the human being has for self-deception. By self-deception one need not mean to make a moral charge. The lie is not a venomous thing, but deeper. It is an ontic thing, invading our very being. Self-deception is primarily the personality's way of shielding from itself the distressing consequences of not knowing who he is. Secondarily, self-deception is our way of shielding from others the erratic adaptation to life which follows upon that ignorance.

The practice of hypnosis has done as much as anything

to expose the capacities in the human being for self-deception. Any living-room hypnotist can repeat the experiments which originally verified the suspicion about the depth dimensions of the self. Organize a party. Pick a subject. Agree ahead of time that when the hypnotist will take him from the room and subject him to the spell, he will inform the subject of these terms: upon awakening from the spell and returning to the room he must not occupy his chair but will lie on his back upon the living room rug! All goes as planned. The subject, defying propriety, confidently stretches out upon the rug. Then the interrogation begins. "Why did you do it? Why did you abandon the chair for the rug?" The members of the party ought to be prepared to hear, without consternation, a very plausible line of reasoning. "Well, as you know, over-stuffed chairs are bad for spines, and I'm saving my back for eighteen holes tomorrow!" Perfectly convincing! Or, "Why isolate oneself at the fringe when he can be at the center!" Even better! But all the while the party knows that these are *not* the reasons which now dominate the subject's behavior. Rather, he is the victim of a direction from another which has seized him at a level of his being which is at the moment inaccessible to himself. Even while dominating him, his motive is inaccessible to him. Yet he can supply perfectly rational explanations for his behavior. The comical thing about it is that the explanations have absolutely no correlation with the real motives. It is astonishing, in the light of all that is now known about the unconscious sources of motivation, to contemplate the extent to which people are going about accepting plausible explanations for behavior which is really in the thrall of deeply irrational forces. What else but this has Christian theology meant traditionally by "original sin"?

With some such understanding of the self's talent for adjustment to life, one is prepared to see the personality types paraded through the anxiety producing situations of life. First, the cosmic situation. The rebellious self sets up a concept of himself as provided for. Because he identifies himself with his concept, he can entertain no suggestion that he is failing in his relation to the world. Hence, he builds bigger and bigger barns, not because he has larger and larger crops, but because he simply must have about him the signs of success. He is what the Bible calls the "worldly" man. The recessive self has the same concept of himself as provided for, but it is held only as an ideal, a goal. The goal seems so far off, he is overcome by the fear that he will fail to achieve it. Hence, he becomes a cynic. By cynic I do not mean what is popularly meant by the term—one who looks down his nose at noble causes. I mean what is meant in ancient Greece. Diogenes was a cynic, not because he went looking for an honest man, but because he went in a barrel, without clothes. Fearful of the capacity of the world to support him, he became disdainful of the world. His disdain, expressing itself as asceticism, was a rationalization of his cosmic anxiety. He is like the man of the Bible who, having only one talent, buries it from fear. Of course, neither the cynic nor the worldly type is immediately acceptable in society today. That is why deception is needed. The rebellious person takes on the public character of the good provider, whom any woman would be pleased to marry. The recessive person becomes the modest-living man, whom any man would be pleased to have as a partner in business.

The resigned type, which really lives off the sense of the inadequacies of the other two types, is a dangerous type to talk about because it is so attractive. The resigned disavows both the acquisitive tactics of the rebellious and the world-denying attitude of the recessive. He is simply careless. He is the Bohemian. His dress is slouchy, he conducts his affairs intermittently; he wears his shirt open at the neck; he does not clean his room. But society scarcely condones this kind of behavior. Hence, the resigned self parades himself not as careless but as carefree. He is in many respects most enviable. But it ought not be forgotten that there is at the base of his apparent liberty the fundamental tension of anxiety, the tension of his repudiation of other ways of meeting anxiety without at the same time knowing how to meet it. His freedom is not a sign of his adjustment to life but rather of his refusal to enter into attempts at adjustment.

Second, how do these types appear in the social situation? The rebellious self sets up a concept of himself as accepted by others, and he will do everything in his power to see to it that life corroborates that concept. Hence, he is the aggressive type, commandeering every situation with the demand to be recognized. Nothing so soothes the wounds of his pride as the oils of flattery. He must be first. His concept of himself demands it. And when he is only second it is as if he were last. He takes no joy in the news of the success of others, and he will even find it possible to pull the rug out from under others in order to guarantee his own paramouncy. The delightful characterization by St. John of the Cross fits perfectly. "They hate to praise others, and delight in being praised, and at times they lay claim to it as a right; wherein they are like to the foolish virgins who, having allowed their lamps to become extinguished, go forth to seek for oil from their neighbors." But there is a sober side. The power of the aggressive is to be feared, rooted as it is in the emotional weakness of anxiety. For as the philosopher Nietzsche has said, the desire to control others is based on lack of self-control.

The recessive, on the other hand, conceives of himself as accepted, but only in ideal. The gap between what he is and what he hopes to be is so great he is agonized by the sheer suggestion of effort required to fill the gap. Therefore, he rationalizes his failure to acquire social status even in advance of an effort. He is the Caspar Milquetoast, always ready to comply with the requests of others, except of course in instances where they presume too much upon his ability. He is willing to serve in small capacities. He will be the secretary, but not the chairman. It is not because he does not care but because he does not dare to be. The higher the ascent, the harder the fall. While the rebellious is the type that must be the campus wheel, always confronting others with the demand, "Do this for me!", the recessive is the plodding worker who only asks, "What can I do?" And those who live in this dark night of the soul, as John of the Cross aptly describes it, never thinking "that they hit the mark in anything," harbor the secret hope that by being meek, they shall inherit the earth. Hence, the weakness of the recessive can be feared because of its subtle strength. After all, our Lord has said "the last shall be first." Or, as Nietzsche observed in exegesis of Luke 18:14, "He that humbleth himself wills to be exalted."

The implications of these two personality types for social behavior are most instructive. Here character takes on a connotation much larger than morality. It involves the whole structure of the personality. Take the matter of one's erratic sexual behavior, for instance. The rebellious must "have" others in sexual possession because he desperately needs confirmation of his power over others. John Dos Passos puts his finger on this motif in his story, "The Big Money." The hero, who has built his life around the power of finance, cannot get Helen, his fiancee, to marry him. When her rejection seems final, he seeks out a brothel, selects a girl, and says to her: "Take off your clothes! Put on plenty of lipstick! And remember, your name is 'Helen.'" The story reminds me of the confession of a young lawyer. The only time in his life that he ever had sex relations outside of marriage was on the night after his failure to pass his bar examinations. Robbed of this vocational certification of his power, he sought verification of his concept of himself in an erratic sex act.

But the recessive self behaves just as erratically, only for different reasons. He must be "had" by others, sexually, simply because he is desperately in need of confirmation that he is lovable. How else does one explain the phenomenal bedroom exploits of a Don Juan. Hyper-sexuality? An old wives' tale compared with the psychological mechanisms illuminated in the recessive type. He will take the confirmation of his lovableness wherever he can get it, so he goes from woman to woman like a bee to flowers.

One need not draw upon such pornographic instances for the illustration of this type. The promiscuity complex shows itself in other than sexual behavior. Take, for instance, the matter of participation in extra-curricular activities or church and civic enterprises. Some people simply cannot say "no" when invited to assume responsibilities.

What is said here should in no way be construed as discrediting school spirit, patriotism, and the wholesome sense of extra social responsibility. Yet one ought not leave his life unexamined at this point when he finds that he is being driven to say "yes" beyond any humane expectation. It is possible that one's concept one has of himself requires that he assume heavy responsibility. Either he esteems himself as having power over others, or he continuously requires the sense that others need him. Either motive makes for promiscuity in social relations. One seduces responsibilities, the other is seduced by them.

Procrastination is another popular anxiety phenomenon in the social situation. Why is it that some people persistently fail to meet deadlines? There are two plausible reasons. One who has adopted the mechanism of the rebellious has a concept of himself as excelling, and he will not submit his finished work until he can bring it into correspondence with his concept of himself. The recessive self is so fatigued by the prospect of illustrating his concept of himself that he can scarcely begin the effort. Both delay: the former to forestall any discrepancy between what he has done and what he believes he can do; the latter because he can barely pull himself together to do it.

The rebellious self, of course, parades as a leader; he can do this successfully, for "the world needs leaders." The recessive type finds his place as the follower, which is as easily done, for "where would leaders be without followers?"

How does the resigned self act? He is the most attractive of all. But do not be deceived by his mechanism. He does not lord it over others and he does not submit himself to others; for he is detached. But his detachment is filled with resistance, the resistance to other methods of accommodation to life. The detachment makes him a most attractive person. Meet him on the campus and he does not try to engulf you in his big wheels with back-slapping "come-ons," nor does he annoy you with recurrent and lilliputian offers of his services. He simply says, "Hi!", and gaily walks on. He is neither a leader nor a follower. He is a "friend."

Finally, there is the ontic situation. Here the personality types get themselves into the gravest difficulties because they are dealing with the deepest realities. How shall one accommodate himself to a universe which holds out an inkling of one's possible being, his abundant life, his meaning and redemption and his durability? The fear that being may not fulfill its promise leads the rebellious to constitute himself as independent of such promises. He will guarantee his own being, and he conceives of himself as just that independent. Hence, he becomes in this situation the atheistic type. It is not that he goes about saying, "There is no God." It is simply that he lives as if the existence of a God would make no actual difference to the on-going of his life. But then this attitude of passive atheism can become an active and rebellious atheism. For if his concept of himself requires him to be independent, the very suggestion of a God beyond himself threatens him and evokes the response of panic.

The recessive self, on the other hand, is so afraid that life will not support him that he begins to kill himself before his time. He is the suicidal type. It is not, of course, that people go around taking their lives in acts of open attack upon themselves. They may simply bite their nails, nibbling away at the outer edges of their lives in some protracted form of suicide. As Balzac has said, "Which of us hasn't killed himself two or three times before he is thirty."

It is possible to illustrate how these types perform in specific life-situations. Note, for instance, their vocational behavior. The rebellious self will stake his immortality on his achievements. Hence, when the papacy tacitly threatened to withdraw the hope of immortality from "The Titan," Michelangelo, he could reply, "I will guarantee my own immortality by binding myself to my work." And he came very close to doing it. The recessive self, on the other hand, is the person who goes to work in the morning not at nine o'clock but at eight, and returns in the evening not at four o'clock or at five, but at six o'clock. You ask him why and he may say he loves his work, or he may even protest how busy he is; but underneath he may be simply "killing himself with work." Ontic anxiety, insinuated into our lives at the point of our vocation, can throw us against the scheme of things and corrode and corrupt us with the elements of eventual defeat. To be sure, few would parade openly as atheistic and suicidal. The customary disguise of the rebellious is in the emulation of Emerson's self-reliant man; while the recessive self is simply the self-sacrificing.

And the resigned self? He is neither atheistic nor suicidal; he is simply fatalistic. "If my number is up," "if it's in the cards!" He is resigned—tense with the repudiation of other alliances with life, but resigned. He is happy-go-lucky, and there is a close relation between fatalism and luck.

It is not unusual for one to flee from this kind of diagnosis as if it were unduly pessimistic. Theology and the health

sciences agree, however, in believing that proper diagnosis
is almost ninety per cent of cure. From the Christian side,
man's dour estimate of his condition is the schoolmaster
that leads us out beyond untenable positions to some more
valid source of hope. For ". . . the man that is will shadow
the man that pretends to be." (T. S. Eliot) One ought, then,
to invoke the conclusion of the British poet, Francis
Thompson.

> "Is not this gloom
> Shade of God's hand outstretched caressingly?"

The truth about man as it is available to us in the Christian faith is an anxiety-reducing truth. I do not say it
removes all anxiety. The spice of life remains. But it removes the unsavory anxiety that makes life tedious and
tasteless. For Christianity is the truth that man is made in
the image of God, and when one knows who God is, the
conditions of reality are present for a salutary adjustment
to the manifold situations of life. To say that man is in the
image of God is to say that man is a being who has the
responsibility for understanding himself as a creature of
God and for conducting his life in that knowledge.

Life in the world can be lived under the knowledge that
the creator is the provider, hence man can know himself
as provided for. Not to know about God's providence is,
as John Calvin has wisely said, one of the greatest miseries.
Trust that the conditions of the universe support our daily
life is so basic it seems banal. But when one sees the fantastic lengths to which the person can go to secure his own
adjustment to life for sheer refusal to choose this knowledge as his own, the basic character of the truth returns at
a high level of importance. One need not retreat recessively

from the world in fear, and one need not seize the world in protean force as if its very endurance depended upon him. "He who when he has the world is as one who does not have it, then he has the world; otherwise the world has him." (Kierkegaard) It is God who gives the world. To know that is to know both that the world is held as a gift and that the gift is assured.

I once overheard three girls arguing about going out in a canoe. One girl refused to go. "Why?" "Because I can't swim," she said. "But the water here never gets over your knees!" the others countered. "I still won't go!" she said. People react to the world with the same irrational panic. The gospels have an answer to every rigid refusal to see oneself as provided for in the world. "Do not be anxious about your life, . . . your heavenly Father knows that you need . . ." These words are the essence of the continuous Biblical witness to the covenant with Noah: While there will be floods in the life of the world, the waters will never rise higher than your knees. The world which God creates He likewise guarantees is navigable.

Life in society can be lived under the knowledge that man is never really alone. There could be small consolation in that truth, of course; for as Jean-Paul Sartre has said, "Hell is other people!" At the same time there is therapeutic wisdom in knowing that the God who is always with us is there to enhance our lives with a sense of status. As Sartre also has said, "Without a looker-on, a man evaporates!" That is, man has an incurable social nature. He is made to be with and for an other than himself. This drive in man cannot be simply traced back and reduced to his life in the uterus, where he learned dependence on his mother. Maturity is a process of liberation from every form of fetal history in the interests of the sole authentic dependence. For man is made for God. To know that the Number One Citizen of the universe keeps us in His attention is the only universally gratifying way to know that there is no moment when our lives are not being dignified. Pascal was fond of observing that the test of a man's emotional strength can be found in his ability to remain alone in his room. The crowded universe of society can be a lonely place even without that test. That loneliness sets up the panic in which the most sophisticated devices are invented to secure our status in society. Aggressiveness and compliance are alternate forms by which we would scrape from the surface of society the gratifications which at last securely rest alone upon the cornerstone of the social structure. That is the stone that no man has laid. It is the redemptive realization that one may cast all such cares on God, "for He careth for you."

Our very life can be lived under the knowledge that every major threat to our being, to our abundant life, is overcome in God. Henceforth, to know oneself in the image of God is to know a life in which every threat of meaninglessness is cut across by the revelation of ultimate meaning in God. Every threat of condemnation is dissolved by reconciliation by God which is revealed in Jesus Christ. Every threat of finitude is countered by the hope of resurrection which does not remove death but does remove its sting and, overcoming death eventually, confers right now upon all life the attributes deriving from the ultimate victory. Revelation, reconciliation, and resurrection are the three R's of the Christian faith. They are all one in Jesus Christ. One can refract them long enough to focus God's intention for man upon each facet of our fracturing life: our doubts, our guilt, and our fears. But Jesus Christ becomes for us what God annointed him to be, namely, "the man that is," the image of God (Col. 1:15) in the time of the world in which that image has been otherwise obscured.

On Thanksgiving Day my family and I were guests for dinner in one of New York city's towering apartments. The festivities over, we started home. The whole family boarded the elevator high over Manhattan. It was already crowded with other over-fed people. On the way down, the elevator stuck between two floors. There was no apparent passage of escape. Impenetrable walls were around us, an abyss beneath us, a pitiless sky above us. There was no great cosmic anxiety, of course. We were all too well-fed for that. There was no real social anxiety, either. We were jammed in with other people, although they did not seem to be the right people in the right place.

From amid the quiet chaos of this situation came one certain note. A little child pursed together his lips and piped a familiar tune.

Adult throats took up the hum, until at last the whole elevator had joined in open song,

> "We gather together
> To ask the Lord's blessing!"

A strange sense of assurance grasped the group. We had the consciousness of everlasting arms underneath. Ontic anxiety was gone.

The image of God in Christ becomes "God's hand out-stretched caressingly." It pursues us in our painful estrangement to reveal the truth about our life with God and to restore us to reconciliation with our true image in God. When man chooses himself in the light of God's beneficent enlightenment, the implosive conditions of our inner life which are the results of the days of our ignorance are winked at. We are then in the presence of the healing that already has begun to make us whole.

THREE

The Crisis of Guilt

"It's not the feeling of anything I've ever *done*,
Which I might get away from, or of anything in me
I could get rid of—but of emptiness, of failure
Towards someone, or something, outside of myself;
And I feel I must . . . *atone*—is that the word?"
                              —T. S. ELIOT, *The Cocktail Party*.

Love bade me welcome; yet my soul drew back,
    Guilty of dust and sin.
But quick-eyed Love, observing me grow slack
    From my first entrance in,
Drew nearer to me, sweetly questioning,
    "If I lacked anything."
"A guest," I answered, "worthy to be here."
    Love said, "You shall be he."
"I, the unkind, ungrateful? Ah, my dear,
    I cannot look on Thee."
Love took my hand, and smiling, did reply,
    "Who made the eyes but I?"
"Truth, Lord, but I have marred them: let my shame
    Go where it doth deserve."
"And know you not," says Love, "who bore the blame?"
    "My dear, then I will serve."
"You must sit down," says Love, "and taste my meat."
    So I did sit and eat.
                              —GEORGE HERBERT, *Love*.

Guilt is a crisis wherever its burden becomes unbearable. Judged by that standard you may think there are not many who bear their guilt as a crisis. Most people do not seem to have so much as heard whether there be such a thing as guilt. That does not change the

39

matter of the crisis, however. For, as Balzac has said, "We cannot examine our wounds; they hurt too much." Guilt is a wound which remains unexamined simply because it is presupposed in the painful experiences of our lives. It burns like a fire hidden deep within the self. The crisis is not in the guilt itself but in the way in which we attempt to handle the guilt. The crisis is in the smoke which curls up from the hidden fire of guilt, choking our effective life and screening off our relations with others.

Mainly there are two critical ways of bearing one's guilt. One way is what might be called the vindictive solution. The vindictive employ a mechanism of self-deception in which others are blamed and despised for faults which really belong to themselves. But if one is a rebellious type personality, he cannot entertain the concept of himself as being at fault. As William Faulkner has said throughout *Intruder in the Dust,* "What sets a man writhing sleepless in bed at night is not having injured his fellow so much as having been wrong," that is, getting found out. It injures the concept he has of himself as invulnerable.

When guilt is experienced by the vindictive as his own, he dexterously puts it off on others. The process can be called resentment: any refusal to accept others which is unconsciously based on one's inability to accept himself. Ivan in *The Brothers Karamazov* sees the devil in his dreams and says, "You are myself with but another face!" The resentful only sees the devil. "Not I," said the Apostle Paul, "but sin."

A man comes home from work at night after a busy day at the office. His little boy meets him at the door. He sweeps the little boy aside, strides into the dining room, and demands his supper. Why does he act like this? Does he hate little boys? No, strange as it may seem, he hates himself. He projects himself into the little boy where he can get at himself, and strikes at himself there.

A political demagogue attempts to eradicate an entire race of people. Why? Does he hate Jews? No, fantastic as it may sound, he hates himself. But the only way he has of striking at himself is to project himself into this group of people where he can get at himself, and to strike at himself there.

How else can one explain the widespread readiness of the public to stamp out evil at the slightest sign of it. Fathom the reign of terror in countries where demagogues announce their hunts for political enemies. The public readiness to hunt out the guilty makes of every neighbor a potential inquisitor. For society demands confession in order, as Strindberg has said, to enjoy delivering the punishment. How else account for the recent public approbation of McCarthyism which alerted the entire populace in the man-hunt for communists. Not alone because we hate or fear communists, but because in some grotesque way we hate and fear ourselves, and projecting that guilt into others, we enjoy the opportunity to spy upon and hunt out ourselves as imaged in others. As a New York Rabbi said during those days, "This is not patriotism; it is paranoia." The paranoic projects into others his own feelings of hostility which are so strong toward himself that he cannot believe it is not someone else attacking him. " 'I have done that,' says my memory. 'I could not have done that,' says my pride, and remains inexorable. Eventually my memory yields." (Nietzsche) Hence, attack upon others is the best defense against their imagined attack upon you.

Hitler after one of his notorious purges is known to have

said while overlooking the shambles of a town, "How wicked these people must be to have made me do this." In such a setting Augustine's words are prophetic. "Do not seek to kill iniquity as if it were something outside thyself!"

Did not Jesus expose this phenomenon when he said to those who had caught a woman in the act of adultery, "He that is without sin throw the first stone"? No stones were thrown. In a moment of lucidity effected by Jesus' action these men came to realize that the sin they were prosecuting was not this woman's sin. It was their own sin projected upon her where they could punish it freely. Jesus' invitation, of course, boomeranged. While the woman went free, eventually Jesus himself was put on a cross and humanity pinned its sins on him. That this is what they were doing was quite unconscious to his persecutors, as Jesus himself acknowledged in his last words, "Forgive them, for they know not what they do." But according to the Bible, Jesus was the one person who could bear the wounds and stripes inflicted by the transgressions of others and in the same act redeem them.

The second popular way of handling guilt is what might be called the self-accusatory mechanism. This is what one experiences when he files his income tax report or goes through customs. He knows quite consciously that his report is fair and he knows he has no undeclared items in his luggage, but when he is faced by the government official, his whole personality slinks away like a guilt-ridden dog. This is one of the main themes in *The Trial* of Franz Kafka. Joseph K. is always under accusation. He never knows the charge against him, but he never disputes its validity. In Dostoevsky's *The Brothers Karamazov* every brother at some time or other pleads guilty to the murder of his father—except the one brother who committed the murder. Almost every day in New York City someone turns himself in for a crime he has not committed. There are even cases of those who will commit crimes, simply to guarantee a punishment they feel they deserve, but for some undetected inner guilt. This is the mentality of those who believe they have committed the unpardonable sin. Where the rebellious cannot entertain the thought of his own guilt because it conflicts with his understanding of himself, the recessive exaggerates his guilt in order to ward off reproach. Posing as the devil, he is only what Joseph Conrad called a "papier-mâché Mephistopheles." The self-accusatory have this in common with the dog, of whom the author Leonard Woolf says, "It does not matter how you treat him or train him, he at once develops this sense of guilt."

Some people feel this is what makes it possible to civilize dogs, while cats, lacking the sense of guilt, cannot be civilized. When a cat has committed a fault, you may look him in the eye forever: he will never admit his wrong. He rather stares you down and makes you feel it is you who are at fault. From the moment he is born, however, a dog has the capacity to put his tail between his legs in self-accusation. The cat is the vindictive type.

A leading veterinarian explored this problem in an address in Chicago recently. *The New York Times* reported the address in a story which carried the suggestive head-line, (Feb. 24, 1957)

EVEN DOGS GET ULCERS
LEADING A PEOPLE'S LIFE.

According to the report, "in big cities dogs, too, are react-ing to the fast pace of urban living. They're developing ulcers." But the doctor was wrong. People do not attack themselves inwardly because of the fast pace of living. It is their sense of guilt instead.

The veterinarian continued by saying that "canine ulcers . . . stem from . . . doubts about food" (a clear case of cosmic anxiety) and "relations with other dogs" (just as clearly an instance of social anxiety)! The real punch of the lecture, however, is this: "Cats, he said, have the answer to modern living that has eluded dogs and humans. They know how to relax." But there he was wrong again. It is not that cats know how to relax. They have simply chosen a different method of handling their guilt. They take it out on others. Dogs take it out on themselves.

The reign of terror in countries which are constantly vigilant for political enemies can partly be accounted for by this tendency. Multitudes who have no slightest taste for subversion nevertheless feel haunted by the fear that it is they being hunted. Hence, the ominous effect of McCarthyism upon the American public. Unnumbered private citizens unknown to government prosecutors felt inexplicably vulnerable. The fact that their personal his-tories were politically unimpeachable did not alter matters. For some reason they felt unworthy and needed to accuse themselves in advance of being accused. Any public move designed to accuse seemed fittingly designed for them.

Joseph Conrad's Lord Jim, heavily burdened by a sense of guilt for a misdemeanor at sea, once overheard a sailor muttering to a small crowd in a port saloon, "Look at that wretched cur!" Jim wheeled around to face his accuser. "Did you speak to me?" Jim asked. But when Jim's eyes followed the direction of the sailor's pointing finger, "he contemplated the wretched animal, that . . . sat with ears pricked and its sharp muzzle pointed into the doorway."

A third way of handling guilt is the method adopted by the resigned personality. The rebellious, unable to entertain the thought of his own guilt, projects it upon others and punishes it there. The recessive seizes it possessively, grinding the heel upon himself in defensive self-accusation. The resigned, however, simply shrugs it off.

Possibly by now you would like to interrupt the whole discussion and complain that it all seems strained and implausible. Well, then, put it to the test. How, for instance, would you react if you were to be told about a pre-ministerial student in a college of your acquaintance who was come upon in his dormitory room having sexual intercourse with a girl friend?

Reaction 1: "Why the dirty so-and-so! He ought to be thrown out of school *and* the ministry!"

Reaction 2: an introspective rehearsal of the history of your own courtship.

Reaction 3: "So what!"

Some of us, you see, can only project our own guilt into the offenses of others; no other explanation can account for the vindictive, almost sadistic relish with which we judge them. Others can only lacerate their own conscience contemptuously, almost masochistically. Still others in sheer refusal to handle the matter in these ways but out of lack of inventiveness for any more adequate way, simply default resignedly.

One can see, then, why Sigmund Freud would counsel not to love your neighbor as yourself. If you did, you would destroy him. Or, one can see why George Bernard

Shaw would warn against doing unto others as you would that they should do to you. "Their tastes may not be the same!" But if you must take Jesus' commandment quite literally, then you would be safest to do it on Nietzsche's terms: "*Do* love your neighbor as yourselves—but first be such as love themselves."

The question is, why do people hate themselves so? These several methods of handling guilt are a direct result of a kind of psychological penitential system in the personality. Suffering from an ill-defined sense of guilt or unworthiness, one develops an acute sense of self-hate which is expressible only in some form of self-punishment. In one case the self-punishment is so acute that it feels as if someone else were inflicting it. In the other case, in order to avert the more painful punishment which attends accusation by others, one probably accuses himself more severely than others would have accused him. The process of self-accusation is a very shrewd one, however. Almost paradoxically, one may attack himself as a defense against attack by others. Through his self-accusation he renders himself virtually invulnerable to attack—a kind of psychological one-upsmanship in which no one can top his self-contempt. He has by his own confession committed the unpardonable sin, and no sin that any one else could dream up to pin on him could be worse than that!

But why do people hate themselves so? Why does one hate himself so intensely that he actually desires punishment? It is a feeling of guilt roughly approximating a sense of unworthiness. "I can't stand myself," he says to himself, and then proceeds to invent the only basis on which he can make his life tolerable, namely, the gradual destruction of himself.

Clinical records are packed with illustrations of individuals who come precariously close to redeeming themselves by self-punishment. There is the case of the penitent forger who cut off his check-writing finger with a butcher knife. There is the case of the father who in a fit of temper struck and injured his child. He immediately fell into a depression and was hospitalized. Patient nursing brought him to the place where he was sufficiently mobile to be employed in one of the hospital's vocational therapies. One day by accident his hand was amputated in a machine. Immediately be began to feel better and his deliverance from depression was in sight. It was as if he had successfully balanced his punishment against his guilt.

Not all self-punitive measures are quite so symmetrical and efficient, and few are so extreme. But without some equivalent to this device, some persons would find life untenable because they would find their unworthiness unredeemable. Many, for instance, find their self-punitive gratification within the social safety of their dreams. There is the case of the young woman who, pregnant for the second time, became deeply depressed. Nightly she experienced variations on one dream: she would be climbing an icy mountain, striving for summits from which, like Sisyphus, she continually slipped back. And always two figures "looked down on her" from the summit: her mother and her grandmother. Her mother had given her a concept of herself as succeeding in a career; her grandmother had given her a concept of herself as sexually pure. The actualities of pregnancy violated both concepts. Depression and the consequent immobilization of her effective life were her psychological equivalents to more physiological forms of self-torture.

Again, there is the case of the young woman who developed a phobia for food. She was averse to anything that might be the carrier of dirt. If the bread in the Lord's Supper could have goodness displaced into it, surely ordinary mealtime food could have badness displaced into it, and she attempted to circumvent that badness by avoiding the food. All food became for her a kind of unholy supper. By her fast she performed an atoning rite. As English and Pearson comment, "In trying to avoid dirt she is ritualistically trying to lead a better life."

Dostoevsky writes with a fine feeling for the human compulsion to bear one's guilt. In his novel *A Raw Youth*, a young soldier confesses to a crime. The court renders the verdict, "No, not guilty." As Dostoevsky says, the soldier "couldn't make head or tail of it. . . . He began to fret, sank into brooding, gave up eating and drinking, spoke to no one, and on the fifth day he hanged himself."

Cases so extreme as these are relatively rare. It would be naive and unrealistic, however, not to recognize their qualitative likeness to the life-disrupting devices universally employed by "normal" people. How many ulcers and allergies are being produced daily in the barter with the unknown God of anxiety? How many husbands are failing vocationally, not for want of skill but for the sheer emotional need to invest in the treasury of merit by sacrificing their success? How many wives are refusing the love of a husband by a fabricated frigidity out of a sheer sense of their unworthiness and the need to punish themselves with unrequited love? People who never give the message of the forgiveness of sins a second thought are capable of ruining their lives in the unconscious effort to bear the burden of their sins alone. People to whom the word "guilt" is the property of courts and churches and who have the need of neither are nonetheless daily sentencing themselves to the miseries of hell by self-contrived penitential systems. Even avowedly Christian people who know the doctrines of their church quite well but apply them only to their "souls," may not yet experience the joy of the Christian life, for they have not lived out its meanings for the whole of life.

What makes a man so unacceptable to himself that he must turn all life into a kind of purgatory? He is unacceptable to himself because he has set up an image of himself which he simply cannot carry off. He feels guilty because he has required too much of himself. He prays,

> "Almighty God! Give me the courage and the power
> To contemplate my own true image without disgust."
>
> (BAUDELAIRE)

He has set up the conditions within himself, however, which thwart the answer to his prayer. And at the end he will probably gladly accept death "to settle an earlier guilt," a "pitiless wedding with a shadowy ideal of conduct." (Joseph Conrad) The gap between his expectation of himself and his real achievement keeps his consciousness continually distraught. The only happiness he seems to be able to salvage is in those moments when his odd sense of justice is being satisfied in some form of self-punishment.

To his failure to be what he projects for himself is added his sense of guilt for the deception he contrives by which to hide his failure. The rebellious type camouflages his failure and the recessive type rationalizes his failure. But while each may fool others by these devices, neither can

shake the unconscious traces from his own mind that this
is what he is doing. Only the resigned personality avoids
the excessive self-hate so characteristic of these other types
because he has not engaged in the self-deceptive devices.
He is equally involved, however, in the problem of how
to cover up his default in self-understanding.

For all types, the problem of guilt is primarily a feeling
synonymous with the sense of unworthiness. It is not the
feeling of anything he has ever *done*. It is some vague
sense of unworthiness, of failure, and he feels he must . . .
atone. The feeling of unworthiness is itself the product
of the personality-formations developed in the anxiety
over how to cope with one's self-identity. In his anxiety
to determine who he is, he has set up a pattern of self-
estimation which intensifies his anxiety by adding to
ignorance the lie, and to the lie the effort to cover up the
lie. Enmeshed in this complex, it seems that there is no
rescue short of wholesome self-understanding; but it seems
that wholesome self-understanding is impossible to achieve
apart from a working through of the problem of guilt
which has resulted from one's faulty understanding of himself. To say it another way, anxiety over one's self-identity
is the root of guilt. This anxiety cannot be relieved, however, except as the anxiety over one's unworthiness is
overcome long enough to expose the real root of the
human predicament.

Is there any hope for the person who is injuring his
effective life by the way he handles his guilt? There is. The
theological answer to the crisis of guilt is found mainly
at two points. The first is simple location and the second
is simply acceptance. Location is what theology has always
known as the doctrine of original sin. Acceptance is what

theology has known as justification by faith. Original sin pertains not to what one has done, but to what he is; not to symptomatic behavior, but to the sources of behavior. Justification by faith pertains not to what one *must* do, but to what God has done which sets one free for creative activity and peaceful relations with others.

This simply means that if critically guilty people are to be helped, it will do no good to snipe at the things they are doing. One must get to the reasons behind what they are doing. And once one has uncovered the source of the behavior, it will do no good to exact further penances or to bring judgment to bear. He has already crushed his life to the breaking point with self-punitive devices of an ingenuity unanticipated even by the inquisition. The Christian answer to the crisis of guilt is to show that the burden of guilt is unbearable simply because man is not meant to bear it himself. Only Jesus Christ is the sin-bearer. Because of him, there is therefore now no condemnation.

Faith, therefore, offers hope to the man in a crisis of guilt. In the first place, as Luther has said, he can *believe* he is a sinner: the problem is too deep to *know*. In the second place, he can *believe* he is acceptable to God through the mercies of Christ: the gift is too undeserved to *explain*. But we can "know by faith" that our fantastic accommodation to life is rooted in our failure to know who we are, made to image the being of God. And we can "know by faith" that we are nonetheless not under condemnation because we can know who God is, the being who has shown Himself in Jesus Christ to be a God of mercy, willing our reconciliation.

There are three good reasons why the sources of our

guilt are not apparent to us, and therefore need to be decoded for us. For one thing, they are too deep. We exist on the basis of our guilt; hence, the examination of it can only presuppose it. The act of the adoption of a concept of oneself and its anxiety formations which result in guilt feelings is similar to a traumatic act. It is our act; it does not happen to us but in and through us; but it has affected us in a way too radical to admit of its conscious recall. It is what theologians call a "primal" act: not simply first in a chain of acts but the source of a chain of acts, itself unidentifiable from within the chain of acts which emerge from it. Acts so original as this put us in the position of the man who has lost his glasses. With that event, we have lost the capacity to find ourselves again.

A second and more instructive reason that our primal acts are lost to our memories is that they are acts which take place in freedom. Now freedom is not simply the rational and conscious capacity to choose between clear and distinct alternatives. Freedom is the power to choose one's concept of himself, the power to determine one's ultimate destiny. But an ultimate destiny is never clear and distinct. If it were, it would be no alternative. It would be a fate, victimizing our freedom mechanically and sapping its quick root of vitality before ever it could be put in operation. It is the *power* in freedom, not simply the choice, which gives our freedom trouble. The power to determine one's destiny carries within it the seed of rivalry against the Reality who first constituted us free and for whom our freedom is intended. For the power of freedom is our most God-like power, and the liberty for self-understanding and self-determination is a talent that goes to our head like strong wine. Heady with the power of a kind of God-almightiness, we act against our true destiny, and when we awaken from our inebriation, we are headed on a path of our own choosing without remembering the conditions under which we chose this route. Our ignorance about the source of our condition, then, is not an accident attributable to low I.Q. or to our sheltered life. Nor is it a necessity of our humanity or of our derivation either from the beasts or from Adam. It is intrinsic in the act itself: in its depth and its freedom. To adopt a line from one of Lionel Trilling's essays, "if we are ill, we are ill . . . by a fault in the economy of our powers, not by the nature of the powers themselves."

The third reason we cannot remember these deep acts of freedom is that the taboo surrounding the act introduces repressiveness. Psychotherapy has made it clear that our acts are apt to be repressive in which we experience a conflict of interest with someone we love who has authority over us. You can rebel against your buddy with complete abandon. But hate rising up against a parent, is not so easy to express. Hate, like steam, must have a vent or explode. Conflict with those we "should" love is held back, pressed down, "repressed." It is unthinkable even to oneself that he would be in such irreconcilable conflict with his parent. Hence, repression is a radical way of saying "no" to and treating as unreal the most forceful drives. In the process two things happen. First, we turn the drive inward where it batters away at us until it finds an escape which can circumvent our sensitive vigilance. But second, which is the point of the reference here, the whole process goes on as if behind our back. We dare not admit it, yet design it so. We are therefore the unknown victims of our own timorous design.

By analogy it can be said that there is no act of open competition with God, our ultimate destiny, which is not in peril of repressive handling. For that destiny is holy and filled with taboo. The free acts committed in such ultimate relations culminate in repressive mechanisms which hide their consequences from us.

But if we do not know what we have done, how can we be held responsible? We cannot be *held* responsible. There is just no point in that. Christianity is not a litigation of the human race; it is a vindication, a therapy, a healing. The desire to *hold* men responsible and to write philosophies of life that conserve the conditions in which they are legally accountable is an intellectual tendency which often participates in vindictiveness and the anxiety-formation of the rebellious. Jesus never held a guilty man responsible. Jesus is not the accuser; Satan is. The early fathers of the church, like Polycarp, were inclined to condemn the *theologically* irregular, but they were almost as gentle as Jesus was with the morally irregular. The total witness of the Christian community is alien to condemnation, for its mission and message is reconciliation. The Christian Church is mobilized to "preach the truth in love." The guilt of man is not the truth; it is the lie. The truth is that God wills to have fellowship with sinners. He does not hold sinners responsible; He holds Himself responsible and takes the consequences of their sin upon Himself. Not to know this about the Christian faith is still to live in the days before Jesus Christ. Not to know this is to have no proper clue to how an early apostle like Paul could at last transfer the basis for his self-understanding to the Christian movement, notwithstanding the shock of conceding that the Messiah was really sent to sinners. Not to know this is to miss the wholeness of the gospel which says that righteousness is a gift and not a requirement.

But what shall we do with the clearly evident judgment passages in the New Testament where God surely holds men responsible? It is as undeniable that these passages are present as it is that Michelangelo has painted a terrifying "Last Judgment" in the Sistine Chapel at the Vatican. But Michelangelo has populated his hell with the faces of his enemies. May this not have influenced his painting of the hand of Christ extended in a gesture of destructive wrath? May it not be just as true that resentment has cracked the clear bell of the early Christian witness to insinuate the bad news of judgment into the good news of God's acceptance through Christ? Surely there is ample basis for this evaluation in the literary and historical backgrounds of the New Testament documents. Judgment passages such as those in Matthew's gospel reflect what scholars detect as ecclesiastical defensiveness, an anxiety reaction to the failure of the risen Christ to return as promised by the church, the desire to bolster morale by holding out rewards for the faithful and punishments for the faithless, and impatience with potential converts who dragged their feet to the statistical jeopardy of the Christian movement.

The fifteenth century, the century of Michelangelo, was also a century of ecclesiastical impatience with the rising indifference of the world to the church. It was a century of judgment and organized resentment. The sixteenth century, the century of Martin Luther, revealed that the wrathful hand of God was a fiction of a man's bad conscience and that the true picture of God is a picture of a God with hands outstretched in mercy. The symbol of the fifteenth century is the penitential stairway in Rome. When one has ascended that on his knees, the Christ at the top of the stairway will receive you in his outstretched arms. A symbol of the sixteenth century has recently been introduced into Italy at the Port of Genoa. Several summers ago "The Christ of the Deep," an eight-ton sculpture of our Lord, was lowered into the sea at Genoa, visible beneath the surface of the water, in memory of sailors who went down in the war. The true picture of the judgment of God is given in the Christ who comes to men. We do not go to him before he comes to us. He comes as the emissary of God, not to require of us but to give to us, and to reconcile us into fellowship with God. Nineteenth-century protestant theology repudiated the notion of a God of wrath on the grounds that it was inconsistent with the notion of a God of love. This thesis cannot be substantiated and twentieth-century protestant theology has shown why. For a God of wrath is only inconsistent with a God who has revealed Himself in Jesus Christ as a God who, while He *could* have chosen judgment, *has* chosen love. God sent His son to save the world, not to condemn it. Because of him there is now no condemnation.

Is there, then, no such thing as responsibility in the Christian life? One need not conclude that from the foregoing remarks. For there are still two kinds of responsibility, neither of which has anything to do with the pinning of blame and holding men accountable. The first kind is the responsibility implicit in repentance. One repents not as the pre-condition to acceptance by God and not because he has been hunted down, found out, and indicted. One repents because while he has no basis for determining the extent of his blameworthiness, there is still involved in his therapy the willingness to *assume* responsibility for himself. As Kierkegaard says, repentance is *choosing* despair. This repentance is not a maudlin or self-accusatory preoccupation with the conditions of his past. It is the turning point to the future. It is life made possible by the presence of the God who freely accepts him and by that acceptance sets him free. In Christ God assumes responsibility for men and thereby makes it possible for men to assume responsibility for themselves.

That liberty to which one is admitted by an act of responsible repentance is the second meaning of responsibility. It is futile to exact responsibility from a guilty man. He lacks the mobility to assume it. For his guilt is not a legal accountability but an emotional brokenness or fatigue. Requirements exacted of the broken only serve to illustrate their brokenness. It is futile to call men to repentance without providing the conditions by which their lives can be responsive. But when these conditions are supplied through the knowledge of God's accepting grace, one enters into "the freedom wherewith Christ hath made us free." This freedom is now the ability to be responsive to the demands implicit in the unconditional love of God. Responsibility, then, is both the willingness and the ability to respond to the invocation of God. The power for both is supplied in the invocation.

If this is really the essential meaning of responsibility, what is there left for us to confess to our priest or to enumerate in our prayers of confession? Has not all the moral fibre been extracted from the Christian life? Has not the clear and structured catalog of sins been reduced to a nebulous theological equivalent of neurasthenia? My

answer to this would be that confession is a highly ineffec-
tive mechanism for promoting spiritual health. Rebellious
types will only confess the sins of others. Their own they
will refuse to confess, for they have a concept of themselves
that does not permit acknowledgment of failures. Recessive
types luxuriate in their confession and by the sheer repeti-
tion of their sins, half of which they invent, they already
begin to achieve a sense of relief. Their self-punitive needs
are satisfied by the very act of accusing themselves through
confession. Thus Dostoevsky says of one of his self-accusatory characters in *The Idiot,* in her "perpetual admission
of guilt she probably finds some unnatural satisfaction—
as though she were revenging herself upon someone." The
self-accusatory are like society women who regularly subject themselves to suffering in order to make themselves
beautiful. It is always a losing battle. Confession based
on the need for self-punishment is an insatiable maw. One
needs it as badly tomorrow as he did today. Hence, some
men confess as thirsty men drink. Confession, being inter-
nally connected with their conceit, can bring no relief to
their soul. The only therapeutic confession is the confession
not to what you have done but to who you are. As Max
Scheler has said, you confess not "I have done this" but
"I could do this." You do not detail your deviltry; you
come to yourself. But this kind of confession is in counter-
point with adoration, which is the acknowledgment of
who God is. These two together establish your true identity
and provide the wholesome basis for pursuing life without
erratic behavior. Freedom from erratic behavior is a consequence and not a precondition of interior wholeness
and harmony with God.

Does not this view of responsibility come into open

conflict with the conscience? Does not the conscience keep
us reminded of our faults and prompt us to confession?
Yes, the conscience (popularly conceived) is as ready to
condemn us as our most malicious enemy would be. Our
conscience is a "prattler," bent less upon our regeneration
than upon our destruction. It feigns an alliance with us
only in the sense that in the administration of punishment
it helps us to satisfy our sense of need for punishment. But
it is a very misleading instrument for a wholesome understanding of oneself. It is not, as one often thinks it is, an
island of purity in our sea of guilt. It is inundated in our
guilt. It is not a seed of goodness, alive within our dying
life, the sole remaining possibility within us for our ger-
mination into newness of life. It is our executioner, bent
upon our destruction, only confirming our lie about ourselves and hiding from us the truth that we are in God's
image, made to be responsible not to our conscience but
to Him. By listening to its chattering fears we have lost
both our eyes and ears. (George Herbert) And when we
know what God is saying to us, we know that we must
choose between our conscience and Him, for the messages
are contradictory. Where our conscience talks us down,
God builds us up. Where our conscience leads us to despair,
God offers us hope. Where our conscience catches us in
moral offenses, God steps between us and the abusiveness
of our own conscience with the gentle words of acceptance,
"Neither do I condemn thee."

But has not God given us our conscience? Undeniably.
But the conscience given us by God and the conscience
"popularly conceived" are not the same. The God-given
conscience is not a moral judge. It is a gauge of spiritual
health. *Con-scientia* and *syn-eidesis,* the Latin and Greek

words from which our word conscience is derived, refer
to a spiritual capacity for discerning our destiny. The
God-given conscience sponsors the intention not primarily
of moral probity but of spiritual wholeness and health.
To "know yourself together," or whole, is the responsibility
of the conscience. To condemn yourself as broken, which
only contributes to your continued brokenness, is the antithesis of the *con-scientia*. To understand conscience as the
agency which holds out the goal of moral perfection and
condemns any failure to achieve it is to define the conscience in terms of a false understanding of oneself. That
understanding is at the root of the lie about oneself which
forces one to camouflage and rationalize every failure to
succeed. A conscience which is God-given holds out a
standard of perfection defined not in terms of ethical idealism but in terms of personal wholeness and health. That is
the promised perfection announced by Jesus in his Sermon
on the Mount as the perfection of the Kingdom when he
said, "Be ye therefore perfect [not as the world defines and
exacts perfection but] as your Father in heaven is perfect."
This verse has served as hatchet-boy for centuries of
vindictive puritanism and self-destructive flagellantism.
Actually in the context of the advent of God's blessed
kingdom which His children will inherit, it holds out the
hope that men will live by God's perfection and not the
world's. The perfection of the world is cruelly exacting,
as any Jew or Greek in Jesus' time could have testified.
But God's perfection is an easy yoke and a light burden
because it confers what it requires, namely, the eye that is
single and the law that is reducible to one word, "love."

Now therapeutically speaking, what difference is there
between saying "Be good!" and "Be whole!"? The answer

to that seems to be that goodness is achieved but wholeness is conferred. Goodness can be required but wholeness
can only be nurtured. Goodness, therefore, is exacted; but
wholeness is promised. The Biblical meaning of righteousness is the therapeutic ground of our ultimate perfection
not a requirement of moral impeccability. Righteousness
rather provides the spiritual conditions for the coming of
personal maturity, wholeness, and health. For righteousness is God's attitude of acceptance toward man which
makes it possible for a man to accept himself and thus to
put an end to the interior apprehensiveness and censori-
ousness which deteriorates his life and his relationships
with others.

Christians are often scandalized by psychotherapists who
seem to relax the moral standard in order to relieve the
tension of their client's anxious guilt. The psychotherapist
in this instance is a better interpreter of righteousness than
many Christians are. There is not a single value to be con-
served by exacting standards of behavior for which the
emotional and spiritual conditions of achievement are
lacking. Moral flexibility may not in itself be healing but
it does less damage than the tightening of the demands
which are already cracking one's nature. There are times
when aspirin is more healing than action. This is the gospel
truth in "the power of positive thinking." As a Bishop of
the Methodist Church once said regarding one of his min-
isters who was in peril of nervous collapse: "There is not
a man in my area whom I can allow to smoke—except
this man; and at the moment I'd let him do anything he
wants to!" The Apostle Paul once said a similar thing:
"Everything is permitted!" Now this was not meant by
Paul as an open gambit to a life of license. His entire

teaching makes it amply clear that the Christian life must
be structured by moral law. But this law is always the
"law of liberty." The difference between the law of bondage and the law of liberty is the righteousness of faith. The
knowledge of oneself as accepted by God sets up a per-
missiveness in our behavior which removes the corrosive
fear of failure and sets us free for creative ethical achievement. By now this knowledge is the property of almost
every pedagogue, parent, and psychotherapist. It is not
easy to administer when we hold that knowledge in sub-
servience to our own resentful or self-accusatory mechanisms. That is why it ought not be forgotten that it is the
essence of a Christian understanding of oneself.

A Christian understanding of oneself as recipient of the
righteousness of God resolves the anxieties which make
guilt a crisis. It resolves the anxiety in which guilt is conceived and the anxiety in which it is intensified. For Christianity tells us who man is. He is made to image God. The
consequence of choosing that understanding as one's own
is to adopt a role that is consistent with the structure in
things. And if one has failed to adopt such a role but has
lived, even if unwittingly, by his own lie about himself?
Then he has a right to know that the God who made us
to image His Reality and to assume responsibility toward
Him also accepts us nothwithstanding the ugly consequences of our lie about ourselves. Because of that, the
burden of guilt built up in our anxiety is lifted. "Who
will deliver me from this body of death? Thanks be to
God through Jesus Christ our Lord! . . . There is therefore now no condemnation for those who are in Christ
Jesus." (Rom. 7:24-8:1) Life seen in the light of the God
revealed in Christ has no place for self-destructive, anxious

guilt. The days of scapegoats, works righteousness, and suffering servants are the days of the old age when it was not yet known that Jesus is Lord and that in him the world is not condemned. Taking your guilt out on others, taking it out on yourself, or simply shrugging it off and letting someone else bear it are all cruel and outmoded means of handling one's guilt. And, to quote a line from Herman Melville, "When a man's religion becomes really frantic; when it is a positive torment to him; and, in fine, makes this earth of ours an uncomfortable inn to lodge in; then I think it high time to take that individual aside and argue the point with him." For in Jesus Christ it can be known that God Himself carries the burden of human guilt, taking it upon Himself. Henceforth our sins are not laid to our charge, for justification is by faith alone.

Manuel Komroff's story, *The Death of Judas,* has a short dialogue between Lazarus and Judas following the crucifixion. Lazarus encounters Judas with the rebuke, "Your face has become loathsome." Judas replies, "The face of every murderer is loathsome. This is God's imprint, the hot iron brand, so that all mankind may know what guilt looks like." But what has transpired here? Lazarus is taking it out on Judas. He has seized upon the treachery of Judas as a dramatic exteriorization of his own sense of unworthiness, of his own involvement in the sin against Jesus, and in punishing Judas he is punishing himself.

Compare with this rebellious handling of the guilt problem the incident in which Jesus announces at his last supper that someone will betray him. "Is it I? Is it I?" they all inquire. Why this reaction? Why not rather protests that treachery would be for them unthinkable? Do they know how possible it would be for any one of them to be the

betrayer? Do they know how close a line there is between
fidelity and disloyalty, how much of the Judas there is in
each of us? Plausible as that may seem, it should be even
more plausible by now to realize that Jesus' suggestion of
possible disloyalty activated their latent self-accusatory
tendencies and sense of unworthiness and led them to accept as fully realistic the suggestion that they, his intimates,
could end his life.

Neither of these stories yet says the last and really
redemptive word about the handling of guilt. Harry Mil-
ton Taylor in his helpful book, *Faith Must be Lived,* reports an incident in the Florida State Prison where for
some years an Easter pageant, "Christus," has been performed. In one scene Judas throws himself before the cross
with the cry, "My Lord and my God, have mercy!" Such
enthusiasm was elicited from the audience by this scene
that it was withdrawn from the play. At the insistence of
the prisoners the scene was subsequently restored, but a
sign was erected requesting "No applause."

The sentiment in this scene comes close to the final
word about the handling of guilt. In one short story
re-enacted in our own experience a luminous ray may
penetrate our lives chasing away every shadow of fear and
condemnation and raising us from servility to liberating
self-esteem. That story we call "Gospel." It is simply
"good news." Knowing who Christ is, no man need bear
his guilt himself, either in self-accusation or aggressiveness
toward others. Christ's acceptance comes not to those who
are already making themselves acceptable by their own
devices. That is fortunate for us. Those oppressed by the
sense of unworthiness have no efficient way of re-estab-
lishing their sense of worthiness. As Paul Tillich has said

quite classically, a Christian is one who accepts God's acceptance of him even though he be unacceptable. God's aggressive love in Christ makes that act possible, accepting us not because of our worthiness but notwithstanding our unworthiness. Such acceptance then becomes the basis for our own acceptance of ourselves.

My wife and I recently returned from an evening out to be greeted at the door by our baby-sitter dissolved in tears. She had dropped our radio and broken it. In a sense she had something to cry about. It was our only set. In another sense we were glad to see her cry, because some baby-sitters would have blamed the whole thing on us; others would simply have passed it off indifferently. Both types, of course, would have done so to their own hurt, for incidents of this sort, while they can easily be forgotten are not wisely handled by that device. They may simply be repressed where they can rise up to haunt us in unconscious but destructive ways. For not all that is forgotten is gone. This girl, however, saddened us deeply. To think she did not know that we were the kind of people who could assimilate this sort of thing!

The truth about man and his self-imposed guilt is that he is harder on himself than God is. For God has shown Himself as one who wills the reconciliation of every man, not on the terms of man's own worthiness but on the terms of His own will to have mercy. That knowledge lifts the burden of our guilt and confers on us the liberating sense of worth.

FOUR

The Crisis of Doubt

"Don't talk to me about God or the saints. I don't believe in your God who took away your legs or wants to take away Michael. I don't believe in your Church and your Holy Mother of God. I don't believe. I don't believe." (James holds out a hand to her, but she draws away from it.) "I wish to God I didn't feel so lonely."

—ROSE IN GRAHAM GREENE'S *The Living Room*.

"When views of religious truth are advanced which either really or apparently differ from such as are commonly accepted, the difference will often be referable to causes that lie back of the arguments by which they are maintained—some peculiarity of temperament, some struggle of personal history, unknown to the public."

—HORACE BUSHNELL, *God in Action*.

Conscientious people worry more than needful over their doubts. Often doubt is utterly inoffensive. In some cases it is even indispensable. When directed against ideas in general, it is no more serious than a parlor game. Indeed, it is a kind of indoor sport. Intellectual ping-pong is an ingredient in every process of thought and it requires doubt for the game. One thinks by setting up ideas and striking at them. According to the rules of the game, doubt is the contender. It must persist until either the idea defaults or until it is pressed to a new and more defensible position. Doubt either worries weak ideas into exhaustion or exercises them into greater strength.

This is called the dialectical method. Dialectic is not a theory. It is a description of how all minds work. (*Dialegein*: to speak between.) In thinking, the mind says "yes," then "no," carrying on an internal debate. The mind, standing above the debate, decides who has it: the yeas or the nays. But the case is never closed. The debate continues at ever higher levels. As the negative voice in the mind, doubt is the attorney for the prosecution, constantly indicting suspicious ideas. In that sense it is as indispensable and inevitable as it is inoffensive. If one says, "I have no doubts," that simply means the game is finished, the court is dismissed, the mind has stopped working.

Doubt only risks being offensive when it is directed against ideas and attitudes which are fondly cherished. The fondest ideas are the ideas from which we derive our sense of support in life. When these are attacked, doubting ceases to be a game and becomes a battle. But the doubting side of our mind knows we ought not surrender to inadequate ideas and attitudes. So it presses its weight against the ideas to see if they will really hold. This function of doubt is especially relevant considering how habitual our ideas and attitudes tend to become. Were it not for doubt's tireless cross-examination, we would find the inertia of our attitudes carrying us beyond the time of their usefulness. Doubt warns us when the vehicle we are driving is no longer up to the demands of modern transportation. We need not have our breakdown on the road. Doubt periodically x-rays the bone of our contentions so that our fractures can be scrutinized before they immobilize us. Ideas and beliefs have what Ortega y Gasset has called an orthopaedic character. They are always subject to fracture. It is the business of doubt to warn us before the load of life breaks them and leaves us in crisis.

This orthopaedic role of doubt is clearly endorsed by the New Testament, and it is a kind of doubt which is completely consistent with a life of faith. Paul, for instance, is "perplexed [i.e. uncertain, in doubt] but not driven to despair." His perplexity is quite understandable, for he is acutely aware of carrying infinite treasures in the earthen vessels of his finitude. The women who encountered the empty tomb were "perplexed [i.e. at their wits' end, in doubt]"; the disciples at Pentecost (Acts 2:12), and Peter, receiving a vision of the Christian mission to the Gentiles (Acts 10:17), had the same reaction. But in each case the perplexity seemed expressed in terms of wonderment: "What does this mean?" (Acts 2:12) Their doubt was a question which fractured traditional ways of thinking and opened their minds to new and creative possibilities. The women shook off their grieving attitude toward the finality of death, and appropriated the sense of the eternal presence of their Lord. The disciples shook off their indecisiveness about the future of their mission and entered into a history filled with the assurance of the leadership of Christ. Peter shook off the sense of the exclusiveness of the Christian community and joined Paul in extending the gospel to the world.

Here, then, is the irony of doubt. It comes as a threat to what we value most. It exposes the excess baggage in our beliefs. But it leaves as a liberator in the most redemptive sense. For these reasons it does not pay to regard doubt so anxiously. As Geddes MacGregor adequately demonstrates in his playful book entitled *Christian Doubt,* it may even be that doubt is a part of something so sacred as worship. What else is the meaning of our long liturgical silences if not that in these moments we make concessions to what we do not know and hence give God a chance to speak? Just as surely, doubt is the antithesis of dogmatism of every kind. By creating a cerebral emptiness into which new ideas can move, it saves us from bigotry. A head that is all filled up lacks the intellectual permeability to appreciate a new idea. In a sense doubt even gives us an intimation of immortality. Only God is deathless; hence, we must be willing to hold our ideas as we hold everything else that is mortal—with a sort of tentativeness which concedes to God the right to determine what shall live forever. There is also in doubt a potential basis for ecumenicity. As Professor MacGregor mirthfully proposes, we cannot seem to get together on the basis of what we believe. Why not try to get together on the basis of what we doubt?

Best of all, doubt keeps the spirit of good humor alive and helps us hold our faith sanely. Several years ago a review of Margaret Halsey's book, *Folks at Home,* indicated that Americans customarily have this splendid faculty. They can hold a high ideal in one hand and a wise crack in the other. Doubt helps us laugh our ideas and attitudes out of their rigid seriousness. In the process it helps us cultivate the spirit of adaptability and receptivity apart from which the Spirit of God meets only resistance in us.

There is a precarious side to doubt, however. In fact, it is possible that doubt is potentially a more severe source of personal crisis than any of the other situations. The reason is that in doubt the very meaning of life is at stake. Man's life, being what it is, cannot exist at the level of humanness apart from meaning. And it cannot exist in harmony with the conditions of reality apart from the basic meaning that binds man's life to God in responsibility. For man is the being who is made to image the Being of God. Not to know that is to set off the chain of anxieties which accumulate in the vicious anxiety-mechanisms of guilt. Everything can be doubted—and to man's advantage —except that basic bit of self-understanding. But if doubt is directed against that, corrosion sets in at the base where it is most apt to be upsetting. Doubt at the top of the head is innocent. At the bottom of the heart it can be an act of metaphysical frivolity. To doubt at the top of the head while believing with the bottom of the heart is inoffensive and often fruitful. But to doubt at the bottom of the heart while believing only at the top of the head is what Paul Tillich calls "total doubt," and constitutes a disastrous suspension of the answer to man's deepest need.

When doubt has weakened life at its foundations, there follows a giddiness, a teetering of the spirit which we have called anxiety. And what we have described as guilt is the sense of falling and the thrashing out of one's arms to break one's fall. When through basic doubt one falls away from God in unbelief, he falls apart inside in anxiety, and is very apt to fall against himself and against others in self-accusatory and contemptuous guilt mechanisms.

Doubt in this sense can be worse than even death. The choice between guilt and death is ambiguous. Some choose death as a punishment for their guilt. Others choose to bear their guilt in hopes of exorcising the demon in death, or to retreat into Hamletism, bearing the guilt rather than fleeing to death which they know not of. But "total doubt" is unambiguously worse than death, for by that doubt the reasons for living have been annihilated.

The New Testament takes an exceedingly dim view of this form of doubt. It is popularly translated as "distrust." If Abraham had had it, he would have wavered concerning God's promises. (Rom. 4:20) James calls this doubt "double-mindedness," "instability," being driven and tossed like a wave of the sea. (1:6) It is the kind of doubt which, far from being an ingredient in worship, is the alternative to worship, as was experienced at the ascension of Jesus: some worshipped, others doubted. (Matt. 28:17) Jesus called it "doubt in the heart." (Mark 11:23)

Doubt, then, is ambiguous. It can be extolled as a hero, a Prometheus robbing the fires of mystery and authority from tyrannical gods and making light and freedom available to man. It can be the paragon of sincerity, the knight in shining armor, unmasking sham and virtuously pursuing the holy grail of authentic truth. But doubt can as easily be indicted as a coward, cringing away from the pursuit of truth out of fear of the consequences, or fear of censorship, or fear of the agonies of search. It can be seen as a tyrant which will not move from cherished positions simply because any change would threaten the paramouncy which one's ideologies guarantee him. Or doubt can be seen as a dilettante, an intellectual vagrant, moving from idea to idea out of sheer emotional irresoluteness, and not at all in the name of a quest. Just such profoundly emotional dimensions underlie the crisis of doubt.

Doubt can be a crisis under two conditions. First, when the desire to believe is thwarted by the fear that belief cannot be justified crisis is imminent. This doubt creates anxiety, as any ambivalence of fear and desire does. Where anxiety is present the conditions of crisis are always in the making. Second, when anxieties direct themselves against the very meanings needed to reduce these anxieties a crisis of doubt has occurred. It is more perilous than the first kind simply because it is deeper, less obvious, thus harder to locate and treat. Doubt that arises out of the fear that beliefs are not justifiable can usually be dispersed at the intellectual level. The deeper doubt which begins in pre-rational anxieties is not a *bona fide* doubt. It is a rationalization or camouflage of other kinds of problems. To vitiate doubt of this sort is a delicate psychological and spiritual exercise.

I.

Let us deal first with the more obvious of the problems.

Doubt becomes a crucial situation whenever its authentic mission becomes glossed over by fear. Fear alone could never ambush doubt. But when fear collides with desire, trouble begins. The trouble is called ambivalence, the equal pressure of two opposite forces. This pressure sets up a self-destructive implosion in the self, which is the psychological basis of the crisis. The desire to believe strides forth in an aura of mid-morning enthusiasm. In roll the threatening clouds of the fear that belief is not possible, and the thwarted desire dismounts exhausted, without even a battle. Now doubt is a crisis when the desire to believe is opposed by the fear that one cannot believe. When the desire to support oneself with something ultimately meaningful comes into collision with the fear that this meaning cannot be supported, anxiety sets in, crippling the faculties whereby meanings are resolutely held.

Desire says, "I must decide life has a meaning!" Fear answers, "There is no justification for such decisions." Desire says, "Life must have a meaning!" Fear responds, "Life is the farce we all have to lead." (Rimbaud) Desire says, "A man who bends down to nothing cannot bear the burden of himself." (Dostoevsky) Fear replies, "The knees were meant to bend but not the head." (Voltaire) Desire says, "The coin is tossed, I must call 'heads' for the existence of God." Fear says, pouncing upon the coin, "Don't look! Who knows? Suspense is so pleasant." (Balzac) Desire says, "It's all or nothing!" Fear answers, "You can't stake everything on one card." (Ibsen)

The emotional implications in this destiny-laden ambivalence are not the same as those in just any old struggle. For here the question of one's destiny is before him, and that question is surcharged with the sense of the holy. Wherever a question is raised in the context of the sense of the holy, a taboo is present. Taboo intensifies the emotional necessity for a satisfactory resolution, feeding the fires of fear. The taboo present to our decisions is the cloud of witnesses: parents, teachers, friends, pastors, trusting counsellors. Their expectant faces look in at the windows of our suspended decision and urge us to adopt the customary way, the faith of the fathers, the viewpoint of the crowd "back home." One dearly desires to adopt the traditional meanings if only to please those one loves. That desire, however, is sharply cut across by the fear that such meanings cannot be justified. There results a sense of panic that our lives are therefore unjustifiable. That conflict between fear and desire makes doubt a crisis.

There is a whole series of such doubt-producing situations in life today. Their thrust is somewhat objective and intellectualistic. They can, therefore, be identified and characterized. Without depreciating their force, I believe they can be parried to the point where the fear of the impossibility of belief is removed. The anxiety which makes this kind of doubt critical can thereby be reduced.

Rationalism is one such doubt-producing situation. Rationalism is the general climate of opinion which constantly trips up the passion to believe with the challenge, "Prove it!" Now, it is a good thing for us that there is such a climate. It prevents us from stumbling blindly into fads and fanaticisms. The human reason is an excellent faculty. It does more than think. It is the overseer of man's integrity. It is the drive in man toward independence. Hence, it resists every kind of slavish authoritarianism. It is the delicately balanced gyroscope of the spirit which keeps us running on an even keel or on a straight course. Philosophies and theologies have from the beginning acknowledged these roles of reason: namely, to keep man free from alien authorities and to admit into one's experience only what confers coherence and unity upon one's life. This is what is meant when man is called a rational animal: he has the talent for independent and orderly action.

Rationalism, however, is a view of life which mistakes these indispensable legislative activities of the human spirit for creative activities. A philosophy of rationalism is a philosophy which confuses man's ability to insist on adequate solutions with an ability to provide them. The freedom of the reason is only the freedom of independent judgment, not the freedom from all binding alliances. The capacity of the reason to order life is the capacity to yield to sources of authenticity which lie beyond the reason.

Reason itself is not omniscient. It does not have the capacity to provide all the guidance for life from within itself. Reason has the power of the keys, but it is not the door. Reason is not *the* key to the mysteries of life; it is a whole ring of keys. Therefore the power of the keys does not pre-exist the door; for the operation of the right key within the reason of man is only really possible when the key is brought into relation with the right door. Reason, then, is made, like man its bearer, in the image of God. This simply means that the reason is not doing what it was made for until it is responding to the existence of God and bringing all its thoughts into captivity to The Door.

The New Testament knows about rationalism and brands it as a way of thinking which blocks faith. It is a kind of reasoning based on calculation. You will find it in evidence in the New Testament where the enemies of Jesus are setting traps for him, or where his friends are vying for greatness in the kingdom. You will notice that Paul admonishes the churches (Rom. 14:1) to welcome the weak in faith, but not the doubter, the disputer. The author of the Letter to Timothy warns against it as one of the obstructions to an effective prayer life. (1 Tim. 2:8) Commenting on that passage in Timothy, Wesley says in his *Notes* on the New Testament, "The sum of our wishes should be, to pray and live, and die, without any ... doubt." If Wesley were ruling out all doubt as hostile to the Christian life, he would be up against it to support his position from the New Testament, as we have seen earlier. Actually, however, Wesley is commenting on this particular kind of doubt, this form of calculated reasoning which weakens one's hold on faith as other forms of doubt do not. The same type of doubt is ambiguously translated

in two verses of scripture which are chiefly responsible for
Christian rigidness about doubt: 1 Cor. 3:20, "The
thoughts of the wise are futile"; and Phil. 2:14, "Do all
things without *questioning*." The Bible is not prohibiting
thoughts and questioning. It is warning here that calculation, a certain kind of ultimately unproductive reasoning,
is hostile to the coming of faith. The best way, therefore,
to handle the doubt-producing situation of rationalism
is to doubt its adequacy for approaching the question of
a meaningful life.

Pragmatism is another doubt-producing situation. Prag-
matism is the sentiment which asks of any belief, "Does
it work? Does it do what it claims it does?" Now, classical
American pragmatism of the William James and John
Dewey variety did not set workability up as a test of truth.
It did not say, "If it works, it's true." It simply said, "You
will only know the truth when it is working for you."
In the classical sense, then, pragmatism is not so much
a doubt-producing situation as it is an experimental faith.
One adopts a point of view as his own, and in putting it
to work experiences its truth.

A crisis of doubt is produced, however, by the more
vulgar, popular form of pragmatism which will experi-
ment with nothing until it has been adequately vindicated
outside one's own experience. It will cross no bridges
which have not been successfully crossed by others. One
can sympathize with this attitude in relation to the matter
of a faith. One may not be entirely satisfied with his own
solutions to the problem of the meaning of life. Shall he
for that reason leap from his own relatively comfortable
frying pan into some one else's rather dubious fire? Should
an alcoholic break with his particular form of security for

the uncertain promises of a religious faith? Shall a person who has structured his whole life around one set of mores and morals abandon that way for another which holds out verbal promises of superiority? Does the Christian faith, for instance, support one's life through times of moral insecurity? Are the prayers of Christians really answered? Can one face pain and even death with courage through the help of the Christian faith?

These poignant questions have a right to be answered. It needs to be said quite honestly, however, that there is no answer to these questions which pre-exists a working faith. As the gospel of John makes clear, only those who obey will know the doctrine. One cannot know a truth to which he has not given himself. In that sense, popular pragmatism is a delaying tactic which can filibuster a life beyond the deadline for authentic resolution.

Scientism is another such doubt-producing situation. Scientism is a technological frame of mind requiring all the dimensions of human experience to come under the methods of the laboratory sciences. It asks, "Can you verify your belief by perceptual tests and measures?" Logical empiricism, which has lately replaced pragmatism as the leading philosophy in the American colleges and universities, is a primary example. I say "example" because it is the symptom and not the source of the technology. If a claim to truth is not as verifiable perceptually as the data of the natural sciences, it is not (philosophically) meaningful: that is the *credo* of the logical empiricist.

Picture, then, the student moving from the chemistry lab to the literature class. How shall he apply the methods he has used during the last hour to the materials he shall face during this hour? No one says he must, of course. But the habit-pattern of the age of science makes it almost inevitable that he will. The people have been unwittingly seduced by the most fabulous spoils system in the history of mankind. Science, our inestimable benefactor, has bought our vote. Our sense of indebtedness is so enormous, we carry the debt wherever we go. Picture, then, a group of citizens entering the church on a Sunday morning. They will pray, hear the sacred scriptures, and participate in their pastor's interpretation. What chance has this faith if the people have carried into the sanctuary the same methods of thinking that have dominated the rest of their week in kitchen, office, and factory?

Scientism is a way of thinking which approaches *all* the dimensions of life with one set of methods, the methods of the exact sciences. This procedure is not intrinsic to the sciences. It is simply the accident of the misapplication of science into which its grateful beneficiaries have been lured. In this sense scientism is the *seductio ad absurdum.* For life is really too many sided to yield its meanings to a single approach. The French philosopher, Gabriel Marcel, has given us a helpful escape from this temptation, for there are two dimensions of life, and not simply one. There is the dimension of the problem which consists in that which is or can be entirely before us. This is called the realm of "having," where science is most efficient. But there is also the dimension of the mystery, of that which is not entirely before us, our loves and loyalties, our faiths and fundamental philosophies. This is called the realm of "being." Scientism would treat all life as a problem which can eventually be solved, like a riddle or cross word puzzle. After science has done what it can, however, there is still the mystery, the realm of being which will not reveal its mysteries to those who make a living out of knowing. Its secrets will be opened only to those who must know—in order to live.

There are so many riddles which science can puzzle out. From a single tooth, Cuvier could reconstruct the skeleton of an entire animal. Nothing in his scientific method, however, could give him access to the secret of the animal, which is its meaning. Cavendish could determine the precise weight of the world. But nothing in his scientific inventiveness could qualify him, like Atlas, to bear the burden of the world. Man cannot live well without an answer to the secret, the question of meaning. This question will not be answered by the scientist as scientist. Scientists know that best of all. Max Scheler is right, then, when he says that the difference between a chimpanzee and Thomas Edison as the inventor of the incandescent bulb is only a quantitative difference. Edison simply knows more than the ape. But the difference between the chimpanzee and Edison as a man who asks the question of the meaning of life is a qualitative difference. "No chimpanzee thinks he thinks." (Auden) Man is not simply a tool-making animal; he is a praying animal, capable of elevating his thoughts beyond the technological realm.

Secularism might also be regarded as a doubt-producing situation. Secularism is the pervasive assumption in our culture that religion is defunct. It is supported by a species of humanism which provides the philosophical justification for secularism. Humanism makes the claim that the world is self-explanatory, faith is the result of failure of nerve, and religions are as Marx and Freud charged, the rationalizations of unsatisfied desires. Questions about ultimate reality are frivolous and pointless, not because there is no such reality, but because nothing more ultimate is needed than the world around us.

This attitude is becoming less and less popular among the intellectuals. It is a rare thing these days to encounter an intellectual who will not acknowledge religion as one of the bridges between man and a meaningful life. Even fewer will assert that for them the bridge is out. I, for one, am apprehensive about this situation. Religion is increasingly the badge of propriety. When the popularity of religion at the university level no longer admits secularism as a live option Christianity will be the loser. For there is no true faith where doubt is not a possibility. The real sadness, however, is in the condition of things where snide asides and sweeping denunciations of religion, sponsored by influential people who are nevertheless professionally unqualified to judge, paralyze religious commitment out of fear of non-conformity. Secularism is perilous in an age of conformity insofar as faith as a bridge to a meaningful life cannot easily remain a live option.

The existence of other faiths is a doubt-producing situation. Religious pluralism is continually on the rise in our orbit of life. Even one alien faith is enough to provoke the damoclean apprehension so often expressed in these words: "What's to say your way is best?" The German philosopher and dramatist, Lessing, was one of the first to voice this problem in the early days of the Enlightenment. In his writing, *Nathan the Wise,* he tells the story of a father who is expected to confer his ring upon the eldest son as the sign of his birthright. Instead, he presents each of his three sons with an identical ring. There follows a long process of litigation to determine which son holds the authentic ring. The wise judge rules that none possesses it. His case rests on a single observation. The unbrotherly conduct of each of the sons during the trial proved that no one of them was his father's true heir.

This story, directed at Jews, Mohammedans, and Christians, carries a rather obvious lesson. It is the lesson of toleration which is based on the familiar assumption that the spirit of religious truth is less significant than the spirit of brotherhood. The validity of the story is patent: no one is so tuned in to the mind of God that he can quote the ultimate truth with accuracy. The falsity of the story, however, is not always so apparent. While a Christian is one who is called to witness to the truth in love, that love is related to the truth and not to the fallibility in which we hold the truth. Christian love is not a love of brotherliness intent upon binding the religions of the world together in a pooling of relative resources. It is love as mission which takes what it believes to be the truth, lodged with the people called Christian, and shares it with others. There is an implicit scandal and offense in that. But it is possible to overdo the scandal. For a Christian ought not make claims for the uniqueness of his faith and he ought not exult in his privileges in the church. To do so would be to treat the Christian faith as an instrument of exclusion. The very opposite is the case. Christianity is a mission of inclusion. The brotherliness of toleration is a second-rate virtue alongside the aggressive love of the inclusive mission implicit in any stewardship of "the Truth."

Finally, *faulty understanding* is a doubt-producing situation. You often hear one threaten, "If that's what Christians believe . . . !" And the imprecation dwindles off into the implication that he will therefore have nothing to do with the faith. In many cases "that" is *not* what Christians believe. Careless thinking or false information can separate a perfectly good sheep from the Christian fold when a little tender intellectual shepherding could save him.

"You say, 'God created the world in six days'? 'In Adam's fall we sinned all'? 'The Bible is the infallible word of God'? 'Jesus is God'? 'God predestines everything that happens'? 'Jesus will return on a cloud in the sky'? If that's what Christians believe, it's not for me!"

But a Christian does not believe these things. The Christian belief about the universe does not refer to its chemical origins. It refers to the inexplicability of the universe apart from the knowledge that God's creative purpose was motivated by love. The Christian belief does not locate the blame for human evil in some first man named Adam. It is more possible Biblically and extra-Biblically to regard every man as his own Adam. To the Christian, it is not the Bible that is infallible, but only God. The claim for the Bible is that it is "sufficient to give that knowledge of God, and of his will, which is necessary unto salvation." (Westminster Confession) Nor do Christians say Jesus is God. They say with Paul the Apostle that Jesus was "designated *Son* of God in power according to the Spirit of holiness by his resurrection from the dead." (Romans 1:4) As far as God's predestining everything that happens, actually what is meant by predestination is not predeterminism. Predestination is the grace by which God calls us into fellowship with Himself. It does not refer to the multiplicity of details in life in general. Furthermore, do not look for Jesus to come riding on a cloud. "Cloud" for the Semitic mentality which is responsible for this suggestion does not mean what cloud has come to mean

for twentieth-century man. It is not a meteorological phenomenon but rather the symbol of the mercy of God
leading His children. To say that Jesus will return on a
cloud means that when history is consummated, God's
mercy will be found to prevail.

How pathetic, then, for one to break with the Christian
faith on the basis of something the Christian faith does
not necessarily hold.

The way to meet these doubt-producing situations is to
doubt them. They are all inadequate because they hold
up criteria for belief which really strike at the root of
belief without themselves supplying some deeper orienta-
tion to the meaning of life. That is why Peter and not
Thomas should be called the patron saint of doubters.
Thomas was a cautious doubter who put external evidences
ahead of a deeply supportive faith. Peter would not stop
short of a faith that would support him. That is why Peter
walked on the water; Thomas settled for evidences which
met the eye. Thomas lived by a faith that remained when
his doubts were dead. As Melville has said, that kind of
faith "like a jackal feeds among the tombs." Peter lived
by a faith which his doubts brought to life.

Jesus pampered Thomas. When Mary met Jesus in the
garden after the resurrection, he said, "Touch me not."
When Thomas met him, Jesus stretched forth his hands—
as evidence. But when Peter walked on the water, Jesus
let him down. I am just waiting for New Testament
scholarship to discover that at this moment Jesus named
Peter "the rock," not for his foundational properties, but
for his sinking properties. This is why Peter is the patron
saint of doubters. He would trust nothing that would not
hold him up. He discovered for us what it takes us pre-

cariously long to discover, namely, that we have no buoy-
ancy within ourselves. Our ability to navigate life is
directly related to our directing our gaze upon Jesus
Christ, who alone supports us.

A student who had visited the Holy Land once showed
me a picture of himself taken right at the point on the sea
of Galilee where Peter was said to have walked on the
water. There was this student, walking on the waters
himself. It was a trumped up picture. He was really standing on a rock off shore. But Peter would settle for no
trumped up faith. He was willing to risk submersion rather
than trust any other foundation than that which no man
hath laid. That is why Peter is the patron saint of doubt.
He endorses a radical kind of doubt which goes beneath
all trumped up offers of support until it feels the solid
rock, the authentic support.

If you have ever visited the chapel at the United States
Naval Academy in Annapolis you know that the stained
glass window in the chancel depicts Peter sinking beneath
the waves, stretching out his hand and calling, "Lord
save me!" As I sat there late one afternoon contemplating
that theme, it was as if I could hear the words of the poet
Francis Thompson:

> "Lift up your head and hark, what sounds are in the dark;
> For his feet are coming to thee on the waters."

As Ortega has said, "doubt is a seascape and inspires in
man the fear of shipwreck." Or as Melville has Ahab say
as he tightens a carpenter's vice upon his hand, "I like to
feel something in this slippery world that can hold." Well,

> "Lift up your head and hark, what sounds are in the dark;
> For his feet are coming to thee on the waters."

II.

Up to this point, the doubt that has produced crisis has been the doubt based on the apparent inadequacy of one's beliefs. They have been *bona fide* intellectual doubts. The best way to meet such doubt is to doubt the doubt until the really basic element in the faith is allowed to provide its own support.

How does one handle doubts, however, which are based not on the inadequacy of beliefs but on the need to be a doubter? What if the doubt emanates not from the top of the head but from the bottom of the heart? What if the apparent reasons for doubt have all been quite adequately met and yet one continues to persist in doubt? Can you deal at the top of the head with issues that are really arising at the bottom of the heart? Can you deal in an intellectual medium with concerns that originate in a deeply emotional or spiritual medium? Is it true to answer questions in a medium in which they do not arise? Is not F. D. Maurice entirely correct in saying, "That which is a tendency and habit of the heart, is not cured by detecting fallacies in the mode in which it is embodied and presented to the intellect"?

People have been known to hold their beliefs in this same way, not because the beliefs are good ones, but because they are the kinds of people who simply must believe. The rebellious, for instance, believes fanatically. He holds his beliefs too tightly. He believes in this assured way not because his beliefs are good, but simply because he is the kind of person who can never be wrong. The recessive believes in a tolerant way. He holds his beliefs too loosely. You can hear him say, "Everyone has his point of view," or, "There are, of course, two sides to every question." What he means is that he would not dare to hold his beliefs in a way that would alienate others. The resigned, of course, does not really hold his beliefs at all; he juggles them. You cannot say that he is an unbeliever, because, like the juggler, every time you see him he has a belief at hand. But it is always a different one. Surrendering to any one belief is too fatiguing for his detached way of life. He is the type which Kierkegaard labeled the intellectual seducer, fondling all viewpoints with equal passion but never giving himself to any.

Would it not be ironical if doubt were the product of similar types of anxiety formation? I say ironical, because in all such cases good answers to religious doubts could never satisfy the doubter. The doubts are rooted not in the need for answers but in the need for doubts. As John Dewey wisely said, "A personal doubt is pathological unless it is a reflection of a situation which is problematic." But when the problematic element has been reduced and the doubt lingers on, the approach to a solution of the doubt must surely shift. Kierkegaard realized this when he observed that doubt is traceable not simply to the mind but to the obstinacy of the mind. Karl Barth realized it when he called doubt not simply unbelief but "hate of the truth" and Pascal when he described doubt as "voluntary illusion." Calvin realized it when he characterized doubt as "the sinful effort to put God out of mind" and charged the so-called doubting Thomas with "obstinacy." Emil Brunner is right, then, to say of that doubt, it is "a form of sin, rightly it is the root of all sin, sin in its original form." For that doubt strikes at the very possibility for a meaningful life, yet with a passion so deep, it cannot be dealt with in any rational way. It is not an intellectual act but a passion. And when doubt is a passion, it cannot be reduced by a simply intellectual act. It must be resolved, as Kierkegaard suggests, by an opposite passion, the passion of faith.

The rebellious, for instance, is too proud to believe. He needs to doubt because his concept of himself requires it. He must surrender himself to no one. He may camouflage his refusal to believe behind the socially acceptable disguise of the quest for certainty. But, as Gordon Allport has said, "It is characteristic of the mature mind that it can act whole-heartedly even without absolute certainty." The rebellious, however, will not be simply sure; he must be cocksure. Furthermore, it is a real handicap to the rebellious that the Christian religion has an ethical base for such areas of life as sex, business, and politics. These could threaten his picture of himself. From his position in society, the Christian demand tends to appear as Nietzsche visualized it, a morality for the sick, for weaklings, and for slaves. Why *should* he believe what attacks his picture of himself as morally and intellectually independent?

The recessive, on the other hand, is too humble to believe. He will surrender himself to anything. That is why he cannot surrender to only one thing. He must keep himself on call by any faith, lest he alienate anyone or any cause from which he so fondly solicits the confirmation that he is needed. But then the very excellences of Christianity are for him roadblocks to faith. For the Christian faith singles him out as acceptable. In Jesus Christ God offers man His own companionship. But the humble finds it difficult to believe that anyone regards him worthily, even though he cannot live at peace without that knowledge. The king sends his messenger into the valley to offer to the peasant the hand of his daughter in marriage. The peasant can only throw the messenger out as one who has come to mock him. He could have been a prince, but his violent humility has cut him off from that possibility.

The proud refuse faith because they cannot concede they need it. The humble refuse faith because they cannot concede they deserve it. But the classic instance of the doubter who needs his doubts is the instance of the resigned person. He refuses faith because he is too indolent and too superficial about life to see why something like faith should be relevant. The problem of meaning is meaningless to him because he will not pay the price to go beneath the surface. But belief is not apt to come to one who does not live profoundly. Unawakened to the seriousness of living, an immature man can see no point in a faith which is meant for adults, for confrontation with life at its deepest levels. He is hollow with irresoluteness, not because the issues of life are too great to resolve. Rather, he has already resolved them with his policy of irresolution.

One cannot help admiring the Spanish matador who refused to continue his appearances in Mexico because, as he said, the lightness and apathy of their bulls had caused him to give an inferior performance. One envies the candor of Vincent Van Gogh who fled from a university education because, as he said, "I prefer to die a natural death than to prepare myself for it at a university." One deplores the gap in the thinking of Cicero, the representative man of his epoch, who seemed to know about everything, except that he did not know whether he could believe in the gods. "Can one *live* like that?" asks the Spanish philosopher Ortega. "One can live, naturally," he answers. "But one lives lost as in a protracted anxiety over death."

Some time ago I saw the picture of a drive-in theatre, packed with cars. My first impulse was to wish that I had stock in that company. On second glance, I discovered every car was empty. The lot was being used as storage space for cars being shipped abroad. Before I could control myself, my mind was drawing an analogy between that lot and the situation in the church. Packed with people every Sunday! But who is *there?* The preacher hears his voice leaving his lips with the profound concerns of the faith. And then he hears his voice return, unaccepted, in the sound of an echo from the hollow chambers of the people's resigned and undiscerning lives. (In all fairness, I must admit that at that drive-in theatre there was nothing showing on the screen!)

Man's life is wretchedly insecure. His doubts are proof of that. But the curious anomaly of life is in the circular situation where the hungry mouth of doubt bites the hand of faith that feeds it. Out of lack of faith a man develops anxiety. He expresses his anxiety in the mechanisms of guilt, which ruin the effectiveness of his life. But doubt is raised as a mendacious block to the very faith which shows the way to liberation from anxiety and guilt. As the modern French mystic Simone Weil has said, "The danger is not lest the soul should doubt whether there is any bread, but lest, by a lie, it should persuade itself that it is not hungry." This is also Augustine's sentiment when he prays the confession concerning his days of doubt, "I would have preferred to have thee defeated in me, to my destruction, than be defeated by thee to my salvation."

How does one cope with doubt at these emotional levels? How does one penetrate a doubt that is rooted in the need to doubt: in pride, humility, and superficiality?

> "Nothing is proof against the general curse
> Of vanity that seizes all below.
> . . . . .
> And wherefore? Will not God impart his light
> To them that ask it?—Freely—'tis his joy,
> But to the proud, uncandid, insincere,
> Or negligent inquirer, not a spark."
> —WILLIAM COWPER, *The Task*, III, line 265.

Now Cowper does not take the familiar position of assuming that all doubt can be approached at face value. Doubt which is emotionally based is not intellectually soluble. But then he implies that a man must stop being proud before God can reveal His light. Does this not throw us back to the attitude which makes of the Christian faith a kind of psychological penitential system? Does it not hold out the sacrifice of such states of mind as pride and negligence as the precondition to faith? Does it not say you must despair of yourself before you can give yourself to God? That you must *want* to believe before you *can* believe? Is this not like solving the problem of divorce by telling people they ought to love each other? Or like overcoming depression by telling people to "cheer up"?

Doubt should rather be approached as a symptom of some deeper spiritual conflict. Doubt does pose a block to faith. But faith itself resolves the doubt when it bypasses the doubt in order to resolve the sources of the doubt, which are the pride, the self-defensive humility, and the insensitivity. Faith is the opposite passion from doubt not because it answers doubt's questions, but because it undercuts the emotional need for doubt. These emotional blocks which make a doubter obstinate in his doubt are rooted in his failure to know who he is, and in the compensatory mechanisms of that anxious ignorance. And faith, telling man who he is, obviates the superstructure of his ignorance, which is anxiety, guilt, and doubt. Faith does not say, "You cannot believe until you cease being proud." Faith wilts the pride by uprooting the need for pride, and in the process liberates the mind from unbelief and doubt.

And just how does faith do this? How does it avoid the very circularity involved in telling the morose to cheer up or the alienated to be reconciled? Here the miracle and mystery of faith is seen at its best. Faith is not primarily an answering of questions at the intellectual level; it is destiny-determining. When it tells us who we are: beings designed to be responsible to God as His image, beings who are in default of that responsibility and living against our destiny, yet heirs of the graciousness of God as revealed in Jesus Christ—when this knowledge becomes the basis of our understanding of ourselves, the spiritual sources of doubt dissolve in the inexplicable change of mind called repentance.

> "We've heard in language highly spiced
> That Crowe does not believe in Christ.
> But what we're more concerned to know
> Is whether Christ believes in Crowe."

Now Mr. Crowe, the doubter, may not have known it, and Samuel Johnson in this little quatrain may not have meant it this way, but the hope for Crowe does not lie in

his believing in Christ. That is fortunate for Crowe, for
he cannot believe. He is too proud. The hope for Crowe
lies in some form of self-realization which will dissolve his
anxious, brittle pride and make him free for faith.

It is just this self-knowledge that is communicated in the
truth that is in Christ. That is why the knowledge of who
God is and who therefore we are, revealed as it is in Jesus
Christ, has the capacity for moving a life to faith even
when it is braced against faith by doubt. This knowledge
can evoke faith from doubters as humor can evoke laughter
from the morose. The answer to bad humor is not "cheer
up." And the answer to doubt is not "have faith." To dissolve bad humor one must tell a good joke. And if no one
laughs? You do not tell him you have told him a joke, as
Kierkegaard slyly proposes. For then he will only oblige
you with a forced twist of his lip but no collateral twinkle
in his eye. You must tell him the right story, of course.
Then his diaphragm will heave with laughter before he has
even thought of laughing. Yet the unanticipated jollity
will come with his own concurrence. Humor is just that
powerful.

But the same sort of power resides in faith, in the story
of who God is and who therefore we are. It is, as Dante
said, the "divine comedy" which reaches into the deepest
levels of our inferno and lifts us up into the highest reaches
of paradise. It must, of course, be the right story, the right
word about God. For faith comes by hearing the word of
God. And, as Mark Twain has said, "the difference between the right word and the almost right word is the
difference between lightning and the lightning bug."

FIVE

The Crisis of Vocation

> ". . . . The fears we know
> Are of not knowing. Will night-fall bring us
> Some awful order—keep a hardware store
> In a small town. . . . Teach science for life to
> Progressive girls—? It is getting late.
> Shall we ever be asked for? Are we simply
> Not wanted at all?"
>
> —w. h. auden, *The Age of Anxiety.*

> "You fool! The best job is the one you have."
>
> —martin luther, *Sermon on Luke 2:8-20.*

Our daily work is an arena in which our justifiability as men is being continually tested. This is not always known or acknowledged because the demands of earning a living seem so much more paramount. Almost anyone can earn a living. But in order to do so he must invest the majority of his waking hours. Into the product of his labor a man must pour what Karl Marx called "congealed working time." That is why most working people are clock watchers. Their lives are like a talisman, a magic skin which they hold in their hands. At every stroke of the clock you can feel the skin shrink, and when the skin is gone, life will be over. One pours his life into his job. That is why the paramount question pertains not to earning a living but to vindicating one's

93

investment of his life. You can appreciate, then, that it is not simply grimness which causes the Frenchman Arthur Rimbaud to cry out, "Human toil! That is the explosion which lights up my abyss from time to time."

Many of the explosive crises in vocational life are utterly situational. Given a little prudent adjustment of the conditions surrounding our work or a little plastic accommodation of our attitudes, the critical element vanishes.

There are clashes of circumstance, for instance. The fact that work is now being widely considered as a universal right bespeaks the deep-seated need of men for a vocation. Let a general situation of unemployment arise, and this basic need to work expresses itself not simply as a fear of starvation but as a frustration of one's essential humanity. Retirement affects men in the same way. A recent advertisement in *The New York Times* for part-time workers brought hundreds of applications from retired men. Strike threats evoke widespread anxiety for the same reason. The loom of industry is the womb of a nation's psychological security. Man is a working animal whose very being is at stake in his handiwork; and when he cannot work, he cannot esteem himself.

Another circumstance is the popular situation where vocational preferences collide with all sorts of distasteful vocational by-products. One does not mind his job so much as the tedium and long hours: what Joseph Conrad once called the "prosaic severity" of daily work. He likes to tinker with motors but not to wash his hands. He likes to sell groceries but he does not like to stack the shelves. He likes to make contacts but not to fill out the reports on his contacts. He likes to do research but not meet classes. He likes to preach but not to call. Or, as in the special case of women, they would like a career but they would also like marriage and motherhood. Vocational life is a kind of package deal: one takes the bad with the good.

Likewise there is a fatiguing competitiveness in vocational situations. He must compete first of all for the job he wants. Once in the job, he must compete with his fellow workers for status on the job. Worst of all, he must compete with himself for the realization of his own ambition for himself. Occasionally the competitive situation is ambushed from deep within one's past where the expectations of one's parents have so dominated one's vocational mind that any independent direction weighs one down with the guilt burden of a patricide.

At times the circumstances of work become such as to raise the question of personal suitability. When this question is raised, the talisman grows taut in our hand and we can peek more deeply into the abyss of our lives. For instance, one may feel deeply destined to be an artist; but who can live on the income of most artists? Or to be a doctor; but who can become a doctor who is not already affluent enough to put himself through medical school? There are not many bank tellers who can escape their cage for a life of aesthetic abandon in the South Seas. But what is the alternative to that for a man whose spirit beats like the wings of a bird against the confinement of his job? He must settle for amateur status in the vocation for which he feels destined to be a professional. As James Agate has said, "A professional is a man who can do his job when he doesn't feel like it. An amateur is a man who can't do his job when he does feel like it."

But what if our sense of destiny is nudging us into a vocation for which we lack the abilities for distinction?

Our destiny is then a devil sentencing us to the most acute confrontation with the fear of failure. Many a young man in a burst of idealism has said to himself, "I would rather be a second-rate lawyer than a first-rate clerk!" There is no quicker way to shrivel the talisman than that. The realities of our talents must be gauged to the demands of a vocation or we disintegrate ourselves with the constant sense of falling short.

Another critical clash which enters into vocational life has to do with moral values. Every worker is by the nature of his job suspended mid-way between the question of the profit of the employer and the question of the welfare of the employee. In some well-ordered enterprises this is no alternative, for the conditions are synonymous. To serve the employer is the best way to serve yourself, or to serve yourself is the best way to serve your employer. There are still many instances, however, where vocational circumstances are such as to encourage the mutual exploitation and depersonalization of employer and employee.

Values also clash when one is forced to choose between a life of service to others and a life of socially acceptable self-interest. Teachers face this in deciding between serving needy, small country schools at less salary and status, and serving relatively well-equipped urban schools at more salary and status. Doctors face it when they must decide between a practice among low-incomed groups receiving inadequate medical attention and high-incomed groups accustomed to the best and able to pay for it. Everyone faces the decision in choosing between gainful enterprises and service enterprises notoriously unrewarding from a financial standpoint.

Once on the job, one discovers a set of mores and morals that jogs his tidy idealism. The office secretary must say "He's not in" when he is. The statesman must declare war, buy favor, and support unsavory riders for the sake of wholesome legislation. The laborer must "slow down" and go out on strike or isolate himself from organized labor which in many respects is industry's conscience.

Probably the most popular clash in all vocational crises is the one that has developed out of society's sheer vocational inertia. According to the Old Testament, work is the device by which God has punished mankind for his unfaithfulness. Since the sin of Adam, man is sentenced to earn his bread by sweat. (Genesis 3:17-19; Ps. 90:10; Job 7:1ff; Ecclesiastes 6:7) Whether God would do a thing like that will be debated by theologians, but there is no room for doubt that much daily work today answers to the description of a punishment. The sheer biological demands of staying alive, or, more lately, of living well, have dominated the history of work. Hence, the question of what the work can do for the spirit of the man emerges too late to answer it efficiently. Men with strong individualistic tendencies get caught in rigid vocational systems. Men with a fine feeling for personal relations suddenly discover themselves being victimized by automation. Men with deep-seated passions to serve their fellow-men come to themselves in jobs whose ends are not apparent beyond the thickly impersonal walls of their offices or factories. Like a dirge, the words of the poet Hölderlin echo through the hollow chambers of these lives:

> "And the wheel of stale usage
> Day by day wears away the soul."

Hell is a job in which a man who lives by his lungs is forced to work under water. It is almost as if the Old Testament were right about work as a penalty. As Simone de Beauvoir has said, "There is no more obnoxious way to punish a man than to force him to perform acts which make no sense to him."

The harrowing crises in vocational life, however, emanate from the deep, subconscious anxieties, the failure to know who we are, the setting up of a lie about ourselves and attempting to prove the lie a truth through the medium of our chief life-time occupations. And if the lie does not come off? The same medium we used as a testing-grounds of the validity of our lie we turn into a torture chamber for punishing the guilt of our detected lie.

A person, who enters into vocational life as if it were the scale of his success, courts the gravest spiritual perils. One who requires his vocational life to vindicate his very being asks of the vocation something it was not meant to give. Students should know about this tactic. Odd how after submitting a paper or completing an examination the student cannot rest with his knowledge of his intellectual acquisitions. He is ridden by curiosity as to how he has done, and he haunts his professors with the question, "How did I make out?" Pride of achievement outreaches achievement and even cripples the faculties by which achievement is come by. The tactic should be familiar to everyone because it was the main device used in childhood. The joy in approbation from one's peers was more pleasant than the thrill of the achievement itself. When a student looks into the eyes of a professor with the same panic eagerness for approval with which a child searches out the eyes of his parent, we have a ridiculously anachronistic situation.

But when the same immature demand for the satisfaction of the pride ideal is carried over into vocational life, the anachronism becomes acutely critical. Is that not the pathos in Auden's lines:

> ". . . . To be young means
> To be all on edge, to be held waiting in
> A packed lounge for a Personal Call
> From Long Distance, for the low voice that
> Defines one's future . . . . The fears we know
> Are of not knowing. Will night-fall bring us
> Some awful order—keep a hardware store
> In a small town . . . . Teach science for life to
> Progressive girls—? It is getting late.
> Shall we ever be asked for? Are we simply
> Not wanted at all?"

Is this not also the tragedy in Conrad's *Nostromo?* As Senora Teresa gasps to Nostromo in her dying moments, "Always thinking of yourself and taking your pay out in fine words from those who care nothing for you." But Nostromo can only reply, "I am engaged in a work of very great moment. . . . I am needed!"

Vocational crisis is in the making when one needs to be needed. The sign of the crisis is the compulsiveness in work. How else account for the mild symptoms called "Sunday neurosis"? Away from the emotional support of vocational approbation, a man is at his wit's end. He may have neatly arranged his time so that it would pass rapidly before he returns to work on Monday. He may have planned the day at a double-header. But it rains. He is lost. He needs to be needed; the Sabbath affords no self-laudatory work; he will anesthetize himself against his need with baseball; the rain washes away the magic drug.

If employed people feel this lack of support on their day off, fancy the torture which retirement inflicts upon the vocationally compulsive. Even worse, can you comprehend the trauma incipient in the disability of a younger person who has put all the eggs of self-vindication in the single basket of vocational life. Case histories are replete with instances of persons unable to pursue their line of work by virtue of a crippling disease or accident, who have taken the attitude that life is no longer worth living.

See, then, the toll that is taken upon the personality when vocational life is set within the pride system. The rebellious seems to aim too high. He entertains only the picture of himself as a success and will resist any suggestion that he is not. He is smugly satisfied with his achievements because they were indicated in his talents from the beginning. The truth is that it is not his achievements which satisfy him but the way in which they vindicate his pride ideal. He can be crushed by failure, not because any particular failure is objectively ruinous, but because failure in any degree is utterly alien to his view of himself. Failure is taken not as vocational defeat but as self-defeat. More often, however, he will not accept the verdict of failure. He will blame the circumstances. He did not "get the breaks"; he did not know the right people; he was victimized by unscrupulous associates, etc. Like everyone else, he has too much to do at work. But he generally is not fatigued because he needs much to do in order to certify his concept of himself as omnicompetent.

The recessive, on the other hand, seems to aim too low. He does so not out of lack of ambition. Actually he keeps himself down so as not to offend others whose approbation he dearly desires. His aim in life seems modest not because he lacks high ideals but because all his ideals are *too* staggering, and in self-defense he must compromise with them. Success depresses him. Hence, the instance of the novelist who, on the day it was announced that his book was a best seller, took his life. Failure cannot hurt him, for when it comes he is prepared to receive it in philosophical self-deprecation. "I am no good," he will say. Not because he believes he is no good, but because he must take that attitude toward himself in order to spare himself the worse punishment of having to hear it for the first time from someone else. He is always fatigued. He should be, for he takes on anything that is asked of him. He needs to be needed. The result is over-work. He will work hard and do many things, but he will reject offers of major responsibility. Like the Texas carpenter, asked to step into the post of foreman, he will decline, saying "Nope, I just want to hue out from the neck down."

The resigned does not aim at all. He is a free lance, a playboy. He is a vocational opportunist, resists the regimentation and routine implicit in vocational life, and seemingly cannot maintain the continuity of responsibility required for holding a job. He may seem well adjusted to his work, because when he is off the job he can play with abandon. He does not take his work home with him. The truth of the situation, however, is that he is simply a playboy. His work is so oppressive to him that he cannot wait to get off the job to flounder freely in undemanding occupations so amply provided by our culture in the world of entertainment and recreation. He is an attractive type because he will not seek his self-solution as the rebellious and recessive do, in such complete seriousness about work. His fault lies in his building his life upon the strategy of detachment from those devices, with nothing genuinely liberating to take their place. He is like a man who is continually breaking jail, but never vindicating himself and settling down.

Now, what is the point of dragging you through this lengthy pathology of the vocational life? Simply to observe what a gap exists between the black swamp of self-torture and aimlessness which one can make of his working life and the view of oneself that is available in a life of faith. The word "vocation" in the history of man has become a synonym for something from which you can hardly wait to get a vacation. "Vocation" in the history of Christianity, however, was the word for salvation. Vocation in the New Testament is God's call to man which delivers him from the assorted tyrannies of the world—sin, death, and the devil—and ushers him into a life of joy and peace. What has come in between to distort the meaning of vocation?

What has happened in the history of Christianity is somewhat parallel to what happens in the Old Testament account of how work came to be a thing to dread. God created man in His own image, and God, the creator, was a worker. Man, in God's image, was therefore designed to be a worker. But, according to the Old Testament, sin entered. Man chose his own image of himself and attempted to negotiate life in that image. He saw himself no longer responsible to God but rather as being like God, with the knowledge of good and evil. The image just could not be carried off. It was not the truth about man, but a lie. One who lies about himself creates a situation where the needs for camouflage and rationalization are so demanding that the opportunities for wholesome self-development are tortuously confined. This tension began

to show in man's work. He worked no longer as a gardener,
as God originally employed him. He worked for bread,
by sweat. Gardening is an occupation in which there is no
difference between the professional and the amateur status.
But when one must enter the sacred fields and forests with
the acquisitive instincts which the struggle for survival
forces upon him, the sweat of his brow becomes a vile
perfume to remind him, if he has the nose to smell, that he
is somehow living against his true vocation.

The New Testament used the word "vocation" to signify
man's salvation. It did not yet apply this word to daily
work. In fact, the New Testament heralded the coming of
God's kingdom which would supplant the world in its
present phase, and, with the world, the daily work required
in it. Hence, no great emphasis was placed on worldly
work in a day when the world was regarded as doomed.

The Middle Ages began to adopt a different attitude
toward work. The kingdom of God, it believed, had
already come in a sense in the form of the church. Therefore, those who worked for the church were doing saving
work, holy work. They had a vocation in the New Testament meaning because what they were doing represented
the redeeming call of God producing in their lives the
effects of joy and peace. Those who were not working in
the church had a worldly work, and their redemption was
contingent upon the holy work of monks, nuns, and priests.
The first systematic presentation of this attitude toward
work was given by Thomas Aquinas in the thirteenth century. But the attitude had prevailed in the thinking of
the church for a thousand years. In summary, the attitude
involved two positions toward work: First, worldly work
is the punishment for sin. It cannot be regarded as having

a redemptive dimension. Second, the holy work is a higher kind of work.

Martin Luther, with no reputation for tact, tolerance, or temperance, broke down the wall between worldly work and holy work with the blasphemous claim that men who worked in the world with their hands were redemptively *more* significant than the so-called holy men, the monks. Luther based his blast upon a hitherto neglected verse from the letters of Paul, 1 Cor. 7:20. In this verse Paul enjoins the early Christians to stay within the calling whereunto they are called. In saying this, Paul apparently uses the same word for one's worldly work as he uses for the divine election to salvation. According to Luther, this is Paul's way of saying that not everything that is holy goes on at church, and with that tiny wedge from the New Testament he broke through the "conceit of the walls" of the church and allowed the church to break into society at this point of very great relevance, the vocational life.

Hear these lines from one of his Christmas sermons, based upon the text from Luke about the shepherds: "And there were in the same country shepherds abiding in the fields, keeping watch over their flocks by night."

"That was a mean job, watching flocks by night. Common sense calls it low-down work, and men who do it are regarded as trash. But the Evangelist lauds the angels because they proclaimed their message only to shepherds watching their flocks by night. . . . And what did they do? . . . They stayed in their station and did the work of their calling. They were pure in heart and content with their work, not aspiring to be townsmen or nobles, nor envious of the mighty. Next to faith this is the highest art—to be content with the calling in which God has placed you." (Roland Bainton's Translation)

Now four things should be said rapidly and pointedly about Luther's handling of this text from Paul. First, his exegesis is wrong. Paul does not say what Luther says he does. Paul only applies the word calling to the life of salvation, not at all to daily work. Second, Luther's position about remaining in one's worldly work became a kind of theological justification for feudalism, with its rigid vocational caste system still so central to the economies of European countries. Third, the Roman Catholic Church has since the Protestant Reformation redefined its position in the direction of Luther's. (See *Rerum novarum* by Leo XIII in 1891 and *Quadragesimo anno* by Pius XI in 1931.) Fourth, John Calvin found it possible to introduce the dimension of saving significance into worldly work without the help of Luther's dubious exegesis.

The fourth point is the important point. The Protestant Reformation helped to make it clear to Christians who were pouring their lives into their daily work that their life of faith was not suspended during working hours. Their vocational life was the arena in which God's calling was to be worked out. The consequence of that perspective was a repristination of work as divinely significant, a concept of the worker not as the victim of evil but as a steward in God's garden.

It is my conviction that when the worker understands himself in his work as one who is in the image of God, under responsibility to God and receiving the benefits of God's mercy in his working life, the crises that come to a head in his vocational experience are sizably reduced. In the main, he learns that his vocation is not the arena for his self-vindication. To think that it is may be bad theology, built upon a doctrine of the fall of man which has not yet heard that God has overcome the power of evil and that there is therefore now no condemnation. It may also be bad psychology, tempting man to seek the gratifications of life from his work, whereas the opposite relation is the more wholesome. One has a satisfactory relation to his work when the worker is a satisfied man.

One who understands himself vocationally as in the image of God will adopt several attitudes of crucial importance to his well-being as a worker. For one thing, he will understand *the essential democracy of all vocations.* The dignity of work does not inhere in the nature of the work. Therefore, people cannot enhance their sense of self-esteem by comparing jobs. The dignity of work inheres in the way in which God is related to the work. As Martin Luther has said, every kind of work has its necessity and meaning in "the command of God." And as Calvin concurred, we are to do everything including our work for the glory of God.

Einstein was wrong, then, to say that if he had his life to live over again he would "rather choose to be a plumber or a peddler" than a "scientist or scholar or teacher." He was, of course, engaging in justifiable hyperbole as an attack upon government security procedures which were crippling scholarly research. He was wrong in the first place to imply the hierarchical inferiority of some work to others. He was wrong in the second place because one does not hold his work as something he has chosen but as something for which he has been chosen. He can only choose his being chosen, and it seems clear that Einstein and others are chosen to be scientists. The father who says, "My son will be a carpenter!" is only kidding. He knows he cannot choose his son's vocation: that would be a contradiction in the term. And he is actually only expressing the disillusionment with professional life which his own frustrations have forced upon him. There is, of course, a kind of hierarchy among vocations based upon adaptability, which vocational aptitude tests are benevolently designed to help us determine. As Alexander Miller says in *Christian Faith and My Job,* "Many heaven-sent mechanics, born in Christian homes, have been turned into doctors to the public danger because of the false status given to the professions." The personal dangers to a vocational misfit are as great as the dangers to the public. Hence, one must applaud the wisdom of Sancho Panza's wife, Teresa, in *Don Quixote.* Sancho, led on by the Don's fancies, confides to his wife intensely, "If I did not expect to see myself governor of an island before long, I would drop down dead on the spot." Or, as most people say, I will become somebody or die in the attempt! The consequence is often a slow process of psychological self-deterioration brought on by failure, the fear of failure, and the corrosive effect of self-accusation. But Teresa wisely replies, "Nay, then, husband, . . . you came out of your mother's womb without a government, you have lived until now without a government, and when it is God's will you will go, or be carried, to your grave without a government. How many there are in the world who live without a government, and continue to live all the same, and are reckoned in the number of the people."

In a day when the public mind gauges one's worth by his vocation, there is psychological and spiritual health in knowing that in God's eyes no vocation is worth more than another. "The best job is the one you have." Or, as Luther also says, "Do not say, 'if I were'; say, 'I am.'"

Does this mean that God is utterly undiscriminating when it comes to varieties of work? Calvin answers that in his comment on 1 Cor. 7:20: "Let no one use this saying to perpetuate modes of life which are plainly impious and immoral." Which means, you do not encourage a bartender, a bricklayer, or a banker to change his job. You simply ask him to take God into it. If there is room, God stays and he then may stay.

Does this mean that God does not call men to specific vocations? It means virtually that. The calling of God is a calling to salvation. It comes to you where you are. The priority, then, is not with the question as to what you should do but with the question as to whether you will admit God into what you are doing. Finding God's will for one's vocational life is like finding His will for anything else. It is plainly difficult, considering the slowness of our spirits, the complexity of life's issues, and the hiddenness of God. The most important thing is not to know God's will but to know that God's will is the most important thing. As the Roman Catholic monk, Thomas Merton, has said in his sensitive way, "Our vocation is not a supernatural lottery but the interaction of two freedoms, God's and ours."

Another redemptive perspective upon vocational crisis is given us in the promise of *deliverance from the moral burden* with which some work ladens us. Nothing so binds us to this world as our work. But the world is a morally ambiguous place, constantly diluting our purest ideals. There are several types of Christian solutions to the world relation, all applicable to our work, but not all adequate. For instance, one may compromise with the world. In this case he will resolve the tension between his standards and the demands of the world by leaving faith out of his wordly work. He will become the economic man, the worldly man. One cannot adopt this solution and still be in the world for *God's* sake.

Or, one may renounce the world. His conflict with the infection of worldly life will be solved by sealing himself off from the infection in some kind of hermetic sanitation. He will do "religious" work; or he will establish colonies for "Christian economics." In doing this, he qualifies as a Christian in the respect that he is not "of the world" but he defaults as a Christian because he is no longer "in the world." A Christian ought not sell out to the world; but neither ought he allow the world to run its course independent of Christian influence. It is obvious that a man may solve his private problem by withdrawing from business or politics, but this kind of monasticism does little to solve the problems of business and politics.

Or, one may attempt a utopian revolution of the world. He will not be a worldly man and he will not be a monk; he will be a martyr. That is, he will demonstrate that he can live in the world of business and politics in open competition with less principled bases of life, endeavoring always to implement the pure ideals of the Christian kingdom. This, of course, sounds like the most heroic and admirable of all the possible positions. It is the "harmless as a dove" strategy, lacking only in the "wise as a serpent" method. Pure ideals in an impure world are precariously brittle. They can be broken in the collision. That, indeed, would be martyrdom. But martyrdom in which the pure ideal is broken by the impure world while the impure world is allowed to move ahead unchanged is socially uncreative. The point about life in the world is not simply to hold high ideals but to change the world. A politician who overplays his high ideals to the defeat of the party may have lost the very implement by which idealism is introduced into society. A businessman who overplays his high ideals may find himself insolvent. Not only is he left without the means for influencing the business world. He is made ironically dependent upon its relief agencies.

Is there a fourth way? Is there an alternative to compromise, monasticism, or martyrdom in one's daily work? There is. One who knows himself as the image of God can know two things about himself: one, that he is designed for work in the world; the other, that even when he is unacceptable to himself, God accepts him. This kind of self-understanding in one's work is the way of justification by faith. One stays *in* the world, willing to be damned by the world for the glory of God, firmly grasping the implements of the world as devices for turning back the world's evil, even at the risk of being compromised and infected by those very implements. Luther's slogan is the battle cry of this method: "Sin bravely!" One can be courageous about his conflict with the world because, as Luther said in his letter to Melanchthon, he can "believe firmly" in the willingness of God to accept even those who are unacceptable. This is not simply a strategy of compromise because it has as its goal the changing of the world. It is obviously not monasticism because it knows it must use the implements of the world in order to effect the change. It is not martyrdom because it knows that most dead men do not move things. One who understands

himself as justified by faith, as living by the righteousness
of God, knows that it is his obligation to change the world
when he can. And when he cannot? He must sin bravely
until he can change the world and in order to change the
world, or until God changes it for him.

Finally, one who understands himself as in the image
of God may bring to his work a kind of meaningful life
which he ought not expect his work to provide for him.
This is what might be called *the internalization of an
external necessity,* to adapt a phrase from Erich Fromm.
Man is a worker. That is ineradicable. And the nature of
work is not always pleasant. It is routine, irksome, and
often meaningless. Men who seek their self-vindication in
their work, therefore, often starve themselves psychologically and spiritually.

In the present complicated phase of society one cannot
always guarantee that work will be meaningful. Nevertheless, Paul's command to the Thessalonian church still
holds for us: "If any one will not work, let him not eat."
(2 Thess. 3:10) Socially necessary work must proceed even
when it is psychologically unrewarding. But then, as
Meister Eckhart has said, "Work does not make us holy.
Instead, we must make the work holy." This is what the
psychologist means by internalizing an external necessity.
We must let our duty become our desire, not depending
for the meaning of our life upon our work, but letting the
meaningful lives *confer* meaning upon our work. Self-
realization was not meant to be the result of work. It is
the indispensable presupposition of work.

Can you sell that idea to the man who stands at the same
machine day in and day out tightening bolts on an auto-
mobile chassis? Or even to a school-teacher, about whom

Strindberg has said, "Teaching is decidedly harder than standing by a screw or the crane of a machine, and equally monotonous"? A man's work is his life, and no man wants to die for eight hours a day. Yet he stands by his machine which raps out its meaninglessness to an iambic rhythm,

> Slĭp túrn slĭp túrn
> Slĭp túrn slĭp túrn

His whole spirit surrenders to the beat of his work, and his life takes on the aspect of a dirge.

> Ŏ cúrse thĕ dáy
> Thăt évĕr Í
> Wăs bórn fŏr thís!

But if a dirge, why not a lyric?

> Shĕ lóvĕs mé
> Shĕ lóvĕs mĕ nót!

Yet lyricism is a form of day-dreaming which merely gives in to one's work or dulls one's senses against its ill effects. It does nothing to transform the moment of work with a meaning that is not implicit in the work. I propose, rather, that the way to transform work with meaning is to let the rhythm of work beat out the meter for a liturgy. Something out of the Psalms, for instance, such as:

> Thĕ Lórd's mў shéphĕrd I'lĭ nŏt wánt
> Hĕ mákes mĕ dówn tŏ líe. (Scottish Meter)

The principle is sound. T. North Whitehead defends it in the essay "Meaningful Jobs for Whole People:"

"In our modern industrial civilization it seems inevitable that most people should be paid workers, and it is of the very first importance that their jobs should be meaningful to them. But I suggest that we shall not get much farther in our thinking if we fix our eyes too narrowly on the job, because what has to be made meaningful is not just the job by itself, but the lives of the workers, both when they are on the job and at all other times." (*Labor's Relation to the Church and Community*, Liston Pope, Editor)

If a man's life is not whole with meaning, there is little his work can do to supply that wholeness. For wholeness of meaning comes when a man understands who he is, the image of God, responsible to His being and the beneficiary of His mercies. *Without* that meaning, the mature demands of our work will only expose the echoing emptiness in our life, or at best, stuff it momentarily with the unacoustical packing of sheer business. *With* that meaning, even the most irksome requirements of work can be transformed into an act of daily worship. The times in which we feel our life diminishing like a talisman can be redeemed by the sense of our affiliation with the only reality which time does not fade.

SIX

The Crisis of Marriage

"The two are sitting at table together; the husband divines nothing of his wife's inner state; they have so little communion that things never even come to a quarrel, an argument, an open conflict. Each of them is so immersed in his own world —she in despair and vague wish-dreams, he in his stupid philistine self-complacency—that they are both entirely alone."

ERICH AUERBACH, *Mimesis,* ON FLAUBERT'S *Madame Bovary.*

"If the glue is good, two pieces of wood glued together will cleave so fast to each other that they can be more easily broken in any other place than where they were joined. God glues the husband to the wife with His own Blood. For this cause this union is so strong that the soul must sooner separate from the body than the husband from the wife."

—FRANCIS DE SALES, *Introduction to the Devout Life.*

The most dramatic crisis of our day is taking place in the institution of marriage. Gradually the frequency of divorce is transforming the structure of marriage into a polygamous form. To be sure, it is only a "one-at-a-time polygamy" and it rarely adds up to more than deuterogamy. It is a social crisis, nonetheless, in which the character of a major institution is on trial.

We are concerned in this series, however, with personal crises and not with social crises. Hence, the question of marriage as a bi-sexual relation will be paramount. I do not mean that the institutional crisis is not urgent and that

114

the Christian faith has nothing to say to it. Quite to the contrary. The wilting of the institution of marriage is significantly related to the flowering of secularism. The secular man is the man who does not lift up his heart. He turns in upon himself. He is the man who in Luther's words is all curled up in himself, *cor incurvatum in se,* "the fabulous wings unused—folded in the heart." (Christopher Fry) In such a climate of life, what chance for survival has an institution whose very essence is in turning outward toward others with self-giving love?

The ingredients for personal crisis in marriage are sufficiently ample, however, to treat by themselves. They are even more obvious in marriage than in vocation. In vocation one must pour his whole life into one job. If he is not whole, the totalitarian demands of vocation splinter his life. Likewise in marriage one gives his whole life to one person. If he is not whole, he cannot be resolute. Resoluteness is the stuff of fidelity; and where fidelity is lacking in a marriage, crisis is incipient. Either the irresolute self fractures the marriage or the imperious demands of marriage shatter the irresolute self.

It may be thought that marriage is one situation that does not answer to the definition of a crisis. It is not sufficiently universal. The fact that one is unmarried, however, or even the fact that one has no intention of being married does not alter the fact that marriage is for that person a crisis. The resolution not to marry no more avoids the crisis of marriage than the resolution not to eat avoids the problem of indigestion. Marriage is indicated for the human race universally in the nature of bi-sexuality. Therefore, all states in life must be defined in relation to marriage.

If one accepts that position, then there are three situations in which the crisis of marriage can be experienced. Here I adopt a classification once suggested by Otis Rice in the *Journal of Clinical Pastoral Work* (Summer, 1949). There is the *broken* situation where the partners to a marriage are separated by reason of divorce, death, or desertion. There is also the *bent* situation which includes all marriages not included among the broken. For all marriage exists under some degree of tension, from the slightest strain all the way to the breaking point. The most serious stage of crisis in this situation is fracture. Not quite broken, yet strained to the breaking point, it becomes a real question as to whether the marriage can be salvaged and even more important whether it pays to make the effort. Amputation might be required in the last analysis. The great bulk of testimony from couples who have recovered from fractured marriages resembles an abstract on orthopedics. Fractured bones which have healed are usually stronger after the fracture than before. There is real hope in that for people who are living through the bent situation.

Many young people, but a great many older people as well, classify in what might be called the situation that has *not yet jelled*. This classification includes a whole gamut of cases. There are those who have every expectation of marriage but are only waiting for the maximal conditions. There are those who are weighing the decision to marry against other socially acceptable ways of life which require celibacy. And there are those whose adjustment to life is so exceptional that heterosexual marriage seems impossible and in some cases even revolting. For all these cases Paul the Apostle has left a reassuring word: "It is better not to marry." (1 Cor. 7:38) This is, as Karl Barth has called it, the "magna charta" of the single person.

Now the fact that I have proposed to discuss marriage as a crisis is warning enough. You can expect that what I say of marriage will not be all sweetness and light. It is the great paradox of marriage that while it is the most idealized of all human relations it is at the same time filled with the greatest perils. Surely you are aware that in the Bible all the evils of the human race are traceable to the first marriage. But possibly you take little stock in these early Genesis stories. Maybe then you will be more impressed by Sigmund Freud when he says: "There is some hatred at the bottom of all relations of affection." But perhaps by now you are unmoved by long-hair psychology. Maybe you will be more greatly moved by the sentiment in the popular ballad sung by the Ink Spots:

> "You always hurt the one you love,
> The one you shouldn't hurt at all."

Marriage is that delicately balanced. Nietzsche could say of it, "One does not know of love who has not despised just what he loved." And Kierkegaard could say, echoing Martin Luther, "Thy wife is first of all thy neighbor, and thou shalt love thy neighbor." It would seldom occur to a young lover to regard his beloved as the object of an obligation to love. And there are not many wives who enjoy being loved as a neighbor, although some men are loving their neighbors better than their wives. But as Luther said, since the wife is the nearest neighbor she should be loved the most. The real revelation in this whole matter is that one should have to be commanded to love the person who in every respect should be the most lovable.

If one does not see that gloomy side of marriage he is
equipped with only one side of a paradox.

On the other hand, marriage is the last human relation
mankind would be willing to vote out of existence. It is
the most sought after, the most filled with the sheer joy
of living, and the most extolled in the finer arts. And in
the Bible, the relation between a man and a woman in
marriage is the continuous analogy for the deepest relation in life, the relation between God and man. In the
Old Testament God is partner to a marriage in which
Israel is the bride. In the New Testament Jesus Christ
chooses the church for his bride. And in that very Pauline
letter to the Ephesians (chapter 5) marriage is virtually
treated as a sacrament. (What Augustine called a *quoddam*
sacrament.) Husbands are to be the head of their wives
as Christ is head of the church. This does not mean, as
many have twisted it to mean, that husbands have a pro-
prietary relation over wives. It means that when people
look at a marriage they should see a visible sign of God's
invisible grace. In the way men love their wives should
be seen the way Christ loves the church. The man who
reminds his wife that woman was taken from the rib of
man should be reminded by his wife that the rib was taken,
as Francis de Sales has said, from the side "which was
nearest his heart, to the end that she might be loved by
him cordially and tenderly." Now when one participates
profanely in the sacrament of the Lord's Supper the consequences, according to the faith of the church, are not
innocent. One does so to his own damnation. And when
one violates the holiness of the mystery (or sacrament, as
the Biblical term can as well be translated) of marriage,
he does so to his own damnation.

The conditions which contribute to breakdown in marriage are synonymous with the profaning of its holiness. I will discuss here five of the most serious of these breaches.

First, there is *exploitation*. When one marries out of love for what the other can do for him, that is exploitation in its commonest and most vulgar form. Karl Marx, who knew a great deal about exploitation, saw this possibility in marriage. As he said, the bourgeoise man has made of his wife a mere instrument of production. It is true that the family, which was made to be an affectional unit, often becomes an economic unit. The love nexus is often displaced by what William James used to call "the cash nexus." Before you know it, the tidy reciprocity symbolized on the bathroom towels by "his" and "hers" has been taken down, and in its place is only "mine," "mine"!

When one marries out of love-for-what-the-other-can-become, that is exploitation in its cruelest form. In this instance, the wife sets up an image of the man she hopes she has wedded. It is really the image which she loves; and she virtually withholds love from the man she has married until he achieves the image she loves. In so doing she sentences her man to a wretched race to achieve the goal which will qualify him for her love. The wretchedness consists not simply in the love fast but in the fear of failure to qualify, which cripples the very faculties by which achievement arrives.

When one marries out of an emotional *need* for the love of another, that is exploitation in its most morbid and diseased form. Now everyone has the right to the love of others and cannot live without it. Man made in the image of God is a social creature. Traditional theology has made much of this. For when God said, "Let *us* make man in *our* image," He may not simply have been using the editorial "we." For God is a trinity of persons, a kind of social nature. And when man is made to image God's Reality, he is involved in the privilege and responsibility of a social relationship.

But love which is a right cannot be required. It must be free to give and be given. Yet if one desperately needs love for reasons of his basic anxiety, insecurity, and emotional hunger, he creates a low pressure area in his personality into which he sucks the love of another to feed his need. This turns the lover into a vampire. True and wholesome married love can only exist where two lovers, each of whom is capable of standing on his own two feet, give and receive each other freely. The rebellious personality exploits marriage because he needs love to feed his omnivorous ego-demand. He has a concept of himself as lovable, and not to be receiving love would jar his self-esteem. The recessive personality exploits marriage for the same reason. He has a concept of himself which leads him to fear that he is unlovable, and he desperately needs confirmation that he is wrong about himself. Not every woman who whispers "kiss me" in her lover's ear is freely offering her love. She may as easily be asking for your stamp of approval upon her uncertain self-esteem. This is not love, even though the side-effects may momentarily feel the same. It is exploitation.

There is no solid basis for marriage in any form of exploitation. Exploitation only stunts the growth of marriage by making love a clinging vine. Like a vampire, it sucks the blood of love while giving nothing. Picture a young couple standing before the altar of the church. She looks up at him as much as to say, "At last I've found

someone upon whom I can depend." But he looks at her
as much as to say, "At last I've found someone upon whom
I can depend!" In a moment you can detect that each is
leaning upon the other and that what they are building
is not a marriage but a house of cards. And then the
minister begins to read the marriage ritual. What he seems
to say is, "Marriage is a triangular affair. For marriages
arc made in heaven. One ought not therefore to expect
gratifications of another which can only finally be granted
by God. One who does not stand erect in the presence of
God in the full understanding of who he is will only lean
against another, forcing him into a role he was never
meant to play. Marriage is based not upon mutual self-
dependence but upon the open reliance of two independent souls upon the God above. That liberating dependence
makes mutual love a life of freedom."

A young lover knocks at the door of his beloved. She
calls from deep within her chambers, "Who is there?"
He answers, "It is I." She replies, "My door does not open
to such as thou." He retires into the desert to mourn, examine himself, and contemplate the mysteries of life.
When he returns, he knocks at the door of his beloved
again, and she calls, "Who is there?" He answer, "It is
thou." The doors of the chamber swing open to him. Saint
Augustine has given us the equivalent of this Persian tale
in one crisp phrase: *"Amo quia est."* No partner to marriage for whom this sentiment is not the dominant note is
emotionally qualified for marriage. "I love her because
she is." There is no reason for love short of this. The
example for married love is set in the way Christ loves the
church: not because it is good, for it is not; not for what
it can become, because he loves it fully now and his present

love makes its future possible; but for no reason at all—simply because it is. No other love is free. There *is* no other love. "O you that are married! It means nothing to say: Love one another with a natural love: two turtle doves make such love. Nor does it mean anything to say: Love one another with a human love: the heathen have well practiced such love. I say to you with the great apostle, 'Husbands, love your wives, as Christ also loved the Church.' And you wives, love your husbands as the Church loveth her Savior." (Francis de Sales)

Another source of crisis in marriage is *an unrealistic view of love*. It is unrealistic to expect that the same sensations surrounding love in courtship will continue in marriage. The love one experiences in courtship is usually a highly romanticized kind of love. For every part of reality in it, there are five parts of fantasy. Jean Giraudoux's play, *Ondine*, recently made this clear to Broadway audiences. In the play a knight meets a water sprite and marries her. The unfolding of the drama is the story of the problems involved in so amphibious a marriage. New York audiences enjoyed the fantasy but did not quite see the point of it all. They did not understand that every marriage is in some sense the wedding of a knight to a sprite. He thinks she is a sprite and she thinks he is a knight, and that romantic moment when sealed by the covenant of marriage threatens to unravel in a story of disillusionment and faded ideals. While the moment of marriage is a highly romantic moment, we do not marry the moment. That moment is ephemeral and cannot endure. As Maurice Valency, the adapter of *Ondine* commented (*The New York Times,* Feb. 14, 1954), "It marks perhaps the acme of our existence, but we do not marry this moment.

Beautiful as it is, it is relatively useless. It does not cook. It does not bear children. It does not help us with our sums or entertain our business acquaintances. We need another woman for that, we need Bertha. This is our dilemma. As men, we love Ondine always, but Bertha is indispensable. We take Ondine into our arms, hoping to find Bertha; we marry Bertha, loving Ondine. And so at every moment we deceive them the one with the other—it is our destiny. And in the end, between them, they destroy us."

The dilemma destroys us, of course, only when we refuse to see the difference between romantic love and married love. Henry James also writes of this theme in his short story, *Madame de Mouvrais*. A woman is married to an unfaithful and abusive drunkard. But to the wonderment of all her friends and neighbors she seems to remain loyal to him. Then one day the husband is miraculously transformed. He conquers the habit of drinking, he settles down into reliability, and he is ready to love his wife again. But she cannot receive his love. It comes about that it is not he she has loved during all this time. She married the romantic ideal and it is that which she now loves. That ideal comes between her and her husband as vividly as an intrusive stranger.

Love and marriage go together like a horse and carriage. But when the love of courtship is hitched to the carriage of marriage, it becomes a horse of a different color. One who does not know that is headed for critical days. "Love," as Balzac has put it in *The Magic Skin*, "is like some fresh spring, that leaves its cresses, its gravel bed and flowers, to become first a stream and then a river, changing its aspect and its nature as it flows to plunge itself in some boundless ocean." Part of the thrill of romantic love is its sheer freedom of escape. Like the fresh spring, it can still decide where it will make its permanent bed. Married love is the end of such freedom, and only mature souls find its boundless ocean a place of endless contemplation. Those who marry the romantic moment find only monotony on the boundless ocean of marriage.

The Russian philosopher, Nicolas Berdyaev, has done modern marriage a service by reintroducing the androgyn myth. According to this myth which was employed by Plato and later by Jacob Boehme, the first man created was sexually complete, neither man (*andros*) nor woman (*gyne*), but both—an androgyn. How then did bi-sexuality arise? When man fell away from God, he fell apart, splitting into male and female. Sin, then, is at the root of bi-sexuality and holds the sexes apart. But the sexes were originally meant to be together, hence the longing of love. To explain the relation between men and women in marriage, two factors must be included and not simply one. There is the longing to be together which explains the attraction in love; but there is a continual wedging apart and resistance which accounts for the difficulty of maintaining married life solely at the level of attraction. It is only a myth, of course, and in some ways more fantastic than the *Ondine* story. But it is deeper. It stands over every love relation, beautiful as it is, with the warning that relations of attraction are constantly liable to subversion. Where that is not known and where one is not prepared to cope with it, marriage can be worn away by frustrated expectations and disillusionment.

A third factor in the crisis of marriage is *an unwholesome view of sex.* By unwholesome, of course, I do not

mean vulgar, obscene, or cheap. By unwholesome I mean
a view of sex which does not see love as a union of the
flesh and the spirit. Any separation of spiritual commitment and physical expression makes love obscene. Man is
a psycho-physical totality. Nothing deeply spiritual can
be experienced without at the same time being deeply
physical. Not to know this is serious for marriage. Ignorance of it accounts for the injurious expression of sexual
love both inside and outside of marriage.

How does it affect marriage relations? When the spirit
is allowed to be separated from the flesh in marriage, either
of two things can happen. Either sexual fear enters to wilt
desire and thwart the love act, or sexual desire enters to
fan the sparks of love into flames which consume. When
the flesh is separated from the spirit it gives the flesh an
opportunity to look in upon the spirit in the love act.
"What!" says the flesh: "express an eternal love through
a momentary physical act?" And in that moment the spirit
feels foolish and comical. Now no one can love when he
feels laughed at. The sense of being comical wilts desire
and freezes passion. But this is the effect of separating the
flesh from the spirit. It produces a condition that makes
for monasticism in marriage. St. Augustine once said that
"freedom from sexual intercourse is angelic exercise both
here and hereafter." But man is no angel. Angels are dis-
embodied spirits. Man is nothing without his flesh. And
love is nothing when it is not communicated through the
flesh. The theologian Schleiermacher believed he could
make love by correspondence. That kind of monasticism
in love is for the angels. The only kind of love that satisfies
the whole man is the love which actualizes itself in the
meeting of skin against skin, a meeting in such proximity

that one has virtually made a covenant by mixing blood.

Lust in marriage is just as unwholesome as abstinence. When the spirit is separated from the flesh the spirit is in the position where it can look in upon the flesh. The spirit becomes a peeping Tom and causes the flesh to sense its nakedness. The feeling of being looked in upon causes embarrassment and the sense of shame. But embarrassment causes the desires to exceed themselves in passion. Passion makes sexual pleasure an end in itself, depersonalizing the object of one's love into a sex object and curtaining off the core of love which is the spiritual commitment. This is what the Protestant pietist Zinzendorf meant when he said, "Right marriage is achieved only where lust is overcome."

Some views of marriage attempt to overcome this dichotomy between fear and desire, between abstinence and lust, by a kind of synthesis of the two. In this view the sexual pleasure associated with lust is regarded as the incentive for entering into a relationship whose real vindication is the propagation of children. But beyond that function no other sexual role can be endorsed. Sex is to the human race what food is to the individual: the very basis of our continued existence. Thomas Aquinas suggested that in both cases, hunger is the incentive. In his colorful and Thomistic way, Bishop Fulton J. Sheen said, in a sermon in St. Patrick's Cathedral, New York City, "The two most important duties of humankind are eating and propagating the human species." "The pleasure" connected with each, he went on to say, was given "by Almighty God as bait, an inducement for fulfillment of a duty," namely, the propagation of the species. (As reported in *The New York Times*, February 26, 1951) When the same sermon on

"The Dark Night of the Body" appeared in his book *Three to Get Married,* the statement was softened, but the same old lines were showing: "The honeymoon precedes the labors of birth, and is a credit God extends in advance because of the responsibilities involved." (p. 252) Bishop Sheen has called this view of sex the "frosting on the cake" view. It is based upon the supposition that the flesh and the spirit are separable, hence it is an unwholesome view of sex which virtually authorizes lust in marriage if the lust serves the ends of childbirth. If one must talk about rewards at all, it would seem that Otto Piper's suggestion is superior. It is child-birth, he says, that is the "bonus" for the sex act, not *vice versa.*

A wholesome view of sex regards the physical act of making love as the visible sign of an invisible spiritual commitment. Child-birth need not even enter the consideration. Sexual love is a spiritual duty. (1 Cor. 7:5) As Francis de Sales has said, "Love and fidelity joined together always produce familiarity and confidence. This is why the saints have used many reciprocal caresses in their married life, caresses truly affectionate, but chaste, tender, and sincere. Thus, Isaac and Rebecca, the most chaste married couple of antiquity, were seen through a window caressing one another in such manner that, though there was no immodesty, Abimelech was convinced that they must be man and wife."

Now a really critical question remains for those of you who are in the situation that has not yet jelled. If deep love must be sexually expressed in marriage, why is it not allowable outside of marriage? I could give you many practical reasons, but I am not your parent. Furthermore, you know these reasons already and none of them is good enough. Let me give you a theological reason. It will not be good enough, either, if you insist on living in defiance of your destiny which is to be in the image of God. Pre-marital love is romantic love which is uncommitted. Like the fresh stream, it still has the option to determine the bed which will thereafter define its boundaries. In marriage, however, as Paul the Apostle has said, quoting Genesis, "the two shall become one flesh." (Eph. 5:31; 1 Cor. 6:16) This makes of marriage "a full communion of life," to use the words of Karl Barth. The sex act is the realiza-tion of full communion. It is a penetration of two selves so intimately that their lives are thereafter indistinguish-able. That is why one who breaks that relationship through infidelity dies. (Lev. 20:10) As Calvin has said, in com-menting on this Biblical attitude, "Whoever divorces his wife tears himself in pieces because such is the force of holy marriage that the husband and wife become one person." Cut marriage in two, and you do not have two pieces, a man and a woman; you have four: a split-in-two man and a split-in-two woman. You do not have two living parts of what was before a single whole. You have four fragments of what could only live while one. Man is the kind of worm who cannot wiggle out of his divorce alive. In pre-marital love the joy of love is still separable from its responsibility. Marriage ends that separation. Thereafter, one finds his joy only within his responsibility.

Monogamy is indicated for the same reason that an extra-marital sex life is not. The King of Siam notwith-standing, it is just as bad for a bee to go from flower to flower as for a flower to go from bee to bee. Most of the reasons adduced for this are faulty because they are cul-tural prejudices with strong pragmatic and pietistic overtones. The New Testament has only one reason. In married love, two bodies become one body. This happens when God chooses the people of Israel, and it happens when Christ makes the church his bride. Marriage is this same kind of unique relation. "Thou shalt not commit adultery" for the same reason that "thou shalt have no other Gods." The sex act is not a mere merging of genitals, then. It is the total identification of oneself with another. One cannot totally identify himself with *two* others.

You may think it odd, then, that I would move from this insistence on the uniqueness of marriage to this fourth situation productive of marriage crisis. I believe that *the legalistic attitude toward divorce* militates against sound marriage. But do not misunderstand. I have not said divorce is theologically permissible. I have said that the prohibition of divorce is hostile to the best interests of marriage. But in so qualifying my position I do not intend to abandon the role of theologian for that of social analyst, and I do not intend to step outside the question of the personal crisis to introduce the question of marriage as a social institution. I simply mean to say that the strict legal prohibition of divorce creates hardships in marriage of a sort that theological understanding need not endorse.

Divorce laws, like all public legislation, keep order in what might otherwise be a chaotic situation in the institution of marriage. But psychologically insensitive divorce laws force couples to live together under conditions of "incompatibility." This is scarcely a meaningless term to those who, having made every honest and intelligent effort to negotiate their marriage beyond incompatibility, nevertheless live on in the cruelest kind of failure. The divorce laws throw a net around the couple and say they must perpetuate their torment. In so doing, they encourage the clandestine affair, the slipping out of the net to find their love "illicitly."

Now Jesus was unalterably opposed to divorce. He allowed no exceptions. Those who divorce and marry again have committed adultery, he said. The exemption in the case of infidelity is an editorial softening of Jesus' absolute requirement. But this is not all Jesus has had to say about marriage relations. He was just as unalterably opposed to looking on a woman lustfully. That, too, is adultery. There are no laws about lustful looks! Of course, the law would have a desperate time controlling the imagination. And who of us would want it to! That's just the point. As Luther said, "You can't keep crows from flying over your head; you can only keep them from nesting in your hair." Or as my favorite radio announcer asked one morning: "Why is a wolf like a railroad train? Answer: You like to hear the whistle even if you're not going anywhere."

Jesus reacted with mercifully good humor in the presence of the woman taken in adultery. He stopped the stoning. But it wasn't the stoning he was against. It was the unyielding character of the moral evaluation implied in the event. Jesus stooped to write in the sand, possibly sketching the outline of the tablet of the law, a sign that the one who shared its authorship should know how to interpret it. Then he turned on the men and not on the woman: "He that is without sin cast the first stone." What did he mean? He had already made it clear in his interpretation of the law. "He that committeth adultery in his *heart*. . . ." That included them all. But he did not condemn them. And he turned to the woman saying,

"Neither do I condemn *thee*. Go and sin no more." The
Christian Church is as much the steward of this mercy as
it is of radical demands.

This, of course, leads us to the final situation to be
considered here, the situation of *irresponsibility*. To quote
the Frenchman, Charles Peguy, "And now abideth liberty,
equality, and fraternity; but the greatest of these is fraternity." Why is fraternity greater than either liberty or
equality? Because you can legislate for liberty and equality,
but fraternity is a spiritual thing which can only be
realized deep within the person. Marriage as a social institution can be shored up from the outside by political and
ecclesiastical law. The spiritual crisis in marriage cannot
be legislated out of existence. Marriage is built upon responsibility, and you cannot coerce responsibility if in
fact the conditions for the ability to respond to another
in faithful love are not present.

Statistical reports on sex practices in marriage are highly
informative. They are limited, however, to the question
of how sex is expressed; they never discuss the responsibility involved in the expression of sex. Statistics about
the increasing divorce rate are alarming enough to attract
the attention of parliaments and congresses, but political
bodies are helpless in the presence of the divorce problem
simply because, as Rudolf Bultmann has said, "He who
divorces his wife has not understood that marriage requires
of him a complete decision."

Marriage obligates two people to love each other irre-
vocably. When two young people appear before the altar
of a church for holy matrimony, does the minister ask
them, "Are you in love?" He does not! He asks them,
"Wilt thou love . . . ?" Married love is resolute love,

responsible love, love shot through with decisiveness and fidelity. But what if one or both parties to the marriage lacks the spiritual mobility to assume that kind of irrevocable responsibility? Irresponsible persons turn the ceremony of marriage into a mock wedding. They *say* they will do what they lack the ability to do.

Visualize yourself being married to the resigned type. You cannot. He (or she) rarely allows himself to form such final attachments. But visualize yourself married to the rebellious type. His (or her) life is dominated by the need to dominate. His guilt sense is expressed by blaming others. If he is a believer, he is fanatical about his belief. If he is a doubter, he needs his doubts as a proof that he is too strong to need a faith. He will love you; and he may love only you; but he will love you with the passion of one who feels all womanhood is coming under his power through his love of you. Or he may not love you constantly. Love-feelings are rarely constant in marriage. But the love-feelings of the rebellious are broken up by the curious projection of guilt upon the object of one's love which makes that one seem unworthy of love and in the moment where love is expected, causes him to turn away. That is the picture of irresponsibility in marriage: the inability to respond with genuine love to the partner in marriage.

Or picture yourself married to the recessive type. His (or her) life is dominated by the need to be dominated. His guilt sense is expressed by the constant blaming of himself. If he is a believer, he is irresolute and insecure about his faith. If he is a doubter, he needs his doubt as a rationalization of his sense of unworthiness for a faith. He will love you, and only you. But when he loves you, you get the impression there is no reciprocity. He is only allowing you to ravish him. It is as if you are not his love but his punishment. Or he may not love you constantly. And why, at the moment of love opportunity, does he turn away so inexplicably? Not because he does not care for your love, but because he does not feel worthy of it. He lacks the conditions within himself for a responsible and reciprocal love life in marriage.

According to the Protestant Church, marriage is not a sacrament. It really ought to be, however. If it is not, then it needs the help of the sacraments. For a sacrament is a means of grace. The sign of a sacrament is the visible communication of God's invisible forgiveness of our sins. No marriage can be fully responsible which does not die and rise with Christ in the holy baptism of the God relation and which is not continually nurtured at the Supper of Our Lord. For no man who cannot accept himself can wholly accept or give himself to another in responsible marriage. The knowledge of who God is and who you therefore are, communicated as it is through the ministry of the church, undergirds marriage with the spiritual ingredients which make inter-personal responsibility possible. Accepted by God, one can accept himself. When one can accept himself, he can receive the love of others and reciprocate with love. Without that spiritual acceptance, marriage may remain precariously cracked. One need not be without it. For the blood of Christ can be the glue of marriage.

Inter-faith marriages are ill-advised chiefly for this reason. When I say, "inter-faith" marriages, I do not mean marriages between Baptists and Methodists! I mean non-ecumenical marriages. Two persons who become one in marriage often find that the one force in life which should nurture their unity really only pulls them apart. Split faiths split marriages. Now couples often solve this dilemma by omitting the consideration of faith entirely from their marriage. This is tantamount to saying you can know each other in the intimacies of marriage without knowing yourself. Your faith tells you who you are and saves you from the self-destructive devices which result from not knowing and from fabricating a recognizable façade for your life. Marriages which are non-religiously based are marriages not so much of persons as of the masks of persons. Under these conditions married life may be, as one says, a real ball; but it is a masked ball. How easy it is, then, to leave one mask and take up with another. But your faith identifies you, gives you a name, and binds you indissolubly to another, all the while providing the adhesive properties for responsible constancy.

Homosexuality, the most poignantly painful and miserably misunderstood of all the human problems, is basically a problem of irresponsibility. Persons who do not enjoy their bi-sexuality are called homosexuals. This should mean that homosexuality is not a difference in kind between people; it is a difference in degree. The Kinsey report helped to make that clear when it revealed how large a proportion of married men and women continue even within marriage to enjoy homosexual practices. A homosexual lacks the ability to respond with complete pleasure to a member of the opposite sex. For some as-yet-unexplored reason, he prefers companionship with his own sex, and holds the other sex off at a safe distance.

By that description, how is he essentially different from men and women who enjoy bi-sexuality but nonetheless hold the opposite sex off at a safe distance? Readers of

pornographic literature, patrons of burlesque, day-dreamers
who reconstruct in their waking hours the lurid scenes invented during their sleeping hours—what are these but
devices for holding off at safe distance erotic involvements
which would be pleasurable were they not so fraught with
responsibility? There is something so impersonal, so *in-
cognito,* so distant about a chorus girl singled out from a
line of curvatious but unknown bodies—and so safe. Married people can be so attractive to unmarried people for
the same reason: their marital involvement is insulation
against your likelihood of involvement. You can enjoy the
pleasures of the imagination without going outside yourself in the responsible commitment of marriage. Or even
within the married relation, you can find yourself caressing your lover in erotic passion and suddenly discover that
you feel the sensation in your own finger-tips; but you do
not feel the skin of the other. Married love can be as
irresponsible as masturbation, even when the acts of
bi-sexuality are being performed. Which is to say that
homosexuality can exist in a degree even within bi-sexually
capable people, because homosexuality is an inability to
respond fully to a member of the opposite sex.

Irresponsibility is never something to be condemned.
Society may be forced to fence it off at times for the public
safety, but even society knows there is no future in fences.
Irresponsibility is something to be cured. The Christian
faith diagnoses irresponsibility as the inability of a man to
respond faithfully to his obligations toward others. As
Augustine put it, if we have fallen out of the creator's
hands, we have broken in pieces. We cannot pull ourselves together for the wholesome response to life which
such situations as marriage require of us. But that is why

marriage is a triangular affair with God at the apex. It takes three to get married in any finally responsible sense. Accepted by God, we begin to become aware of the conditions of self-acceptance which help us to accept others. Without that acceptance, we live in the constant effort to camouflage and rationalize our social ineptitude. With it we are on the way to being liberated for open and wholesome responsibility.

That is why the columnist in a western newspaper was wrong to compare a marriage with the building of a New England town meeting house. The particular town voted to build a new town hall. They decided to build it out of the materials in the old town hall. But they consented to go on meeting in the old town hall while the new was being built. This is *not* what happens in marriage. Something new is added. Into the materials of two lives, God introduces His reconciling grace. That grace is not a buttress thrown up as from the outside which holds up the walls of marriage when the walls are unable to stand by themselves. It is a glue from within, providing the conditions of personal responsibility by which two persons adhere to each other in willing faithfulness.

SEVEN

The Crisis of Suffering

"Think of all the flowers that have come out—the anemones and snowdrops that have to stand in the snow the whole day long—and all through the night, too, freezing in the darkness. Think how they suffer. The night's the worst, because then it's dark, and they are afraid of the dark and can't run away. They just stand and wait for the day to come."

—ELEANORA IN AUGUST STRINDBERG'S *Easter*.

"Her name was Felicitas; she was a Carthaginian; she lay in prison; there she bore a child. In her pain she screamed. The jailer asked her how, if she shrieked at that, she expected to endure death by beasts. She said: 'Now I suffer what *I* suffer; then another will be in me who will suffer for me, as I shall suffer for him.'"

—CHARLES WILLIAMS, *The Descent of the Dove*.

The people for whom suffering is a crisis are those who do not know what their suffering means. But there are at least two different kinds of "meaning." There is the meaning by which one solves the riddles of life. The technological enterprises render that service. There is also the meaning which still remains unexplored after technology has gone the limit. That meaning pertains to some mystery which must still be opened up before the meaning of life is adequately exposed. It is in this second realm that suffering tends to become a crisis of meaning.

The technological approach to life, however, has made

the more dramatic contribution to reducing suffering. When it has viewed suffering as a problem to be eradicated, it has invented the most ingenious devices by which to cope with it. Is the critical element in the suffering the pain? The pharmaceutical industry has largely remedied that problem by barbiturates of one sort and another. In fairness to the human being, of course, it must be admitted that pain never by itself constitutes a crisis of any great proportions. The human tolerance to physical punishment is staggering. Men continue to elect cruel manual labor, to volunteer for torture under conditions of warfare or competitive athletics, and grotesque initiations into tribal councils and college fraternities. Given the proper psychological motivation, mere pain precipitates no crisis. A football coach once gave me the prime qualification for a first-class player: "he must enjoy pain." The sport never wants for candidates who seem qualified. Arthur Koestler helps to reduce public consternation over acts of great physical suffering when he describes how pain was met by victims of communist brutality. "Rubashov," he says in *Darkness at Noon,* "had learned that every known physical pain was bearable; if one knew beforehand exactly what was going to happen to one, one stood it as a surgical operation."

Physical pain is apparently the mildest form of suffering. It is generally associated with the crisis of suffering by those who have seldom suffered. The social suffering which attends physical disabilities is probably a graver form of suffering: "Will my illness force me to lose valuable working time?" But social technology has eased that crisis through insurance and workmen's compensation.

"Can I bear the loneliness that comes with the isolation

of sickness?" John Donne, who has much to say about suffering, placed loneliness high on his list of critical ingredients in suffering: "As sickness is the greatest misery, so the greatest misery of sickness is solitude." But radio and television and benevolent civic and religious organizations have helped to overcome that crisis by introducing social brightness into the gloom of the sick room. Surely even the lowliest of us has had to testify after an illness what the President of the United States observed on returning from a convalescence: "Such a time is not fully a loss. Misfortune brings to all of us an understanding of how good people are."

"Will my handicap force me to be dependent upon others?" But the social technology of this part of the world is rapidly arriving at the place where medical care and hospitalization for young and old alike are being made available, like such other sources of life as air and water, without consideration of economic status.

By a technological knowledge of the meaning of suffering one may even put an end to it. For technology asks for causes, and when the causes of suffering are located and extracted, ill effects wither away. Is the suffering in the body by virtue of such virulent forces as germs and pollens? Then eradicate the germs and pollens. Is it in the mind? Then either it is unreal, in which case one can overcome it by positive thinking; or it is to be attacked through the mind by psychotherapy.

The suffering that remains after the technological sciences have done all they can is the suffering that is productive of the really serious crisis. A man can stand almost anything if he knows it will not last forever, and technology has mercifully abridged the time span of suffering. But what of the suffering that still remains when technologies have reached their limit: the malignancies whose outcome is sure and swift, the disabilities which are as irrevocable as loss of limb, and the curtaining off of sensory channels to a total life? Where in all the technological meanings is there an answer to the cruelest suffering of all, the suffering inherent in the cry, "Why did this happen to me!"

People do not usually realize how they applaud the scheme of things when they register that complaint. Be they petulant or pungent in their response to suffering, when it is framed as a question which draws upon some region of ultimate meaning in life, they are illustrating both the grandeur and the misery of man. It is the grandeur of man that he is able to feel pain. For only one who can ask the question about its ultimate meaning—not simply its technological causes and cures—*feels* his pain in any really critical sense. Animals probably do not feel pain as men do, for they cannot raise the question of meaning. They can eradicate pain through very rudimentary technological tricks. Wolves circumvent briar patches. Almost from the birth of an amoeba, the tiniest creatures camouflage against every attack. Ants and bees can stave off hunger by storing up provisions. Apes administer relatively sophisticated first aid. But nothing less than man can ask the question, "Why?" Hence, nothing suffers as man does the cruel spiritual punishment of sensing an affliction for which he lacks a rationale.

There may even be two kinds of people who never suffer as some men do. If primitive people lack the talent for reflection they cannot give their suffering a meaning. Hence, they do not suffer critically. If philosophical naturalists live by their creed as they profess to, then they *will not* give their suffering a meaning. Therefore they carry their suffering as just one more indifferent incident. In the process each buys freedom from the crisis of suffering at the price of the full privilege of manhood.

While it is the glory of man to be able to raise the question about the ultimate meaning of suffering, not all deliberately reflective men ask the question in the right way. They fail to ask the question in such a way as to receive an answer which will save them from the misery implicit in the question. The key to that fact is that most reflective approaches to the question classify suffering as a "problem." Now a problem, as Gabriel Marcel has said, is the proper realm of the technological sciences. When suffering is treated as a problem it is efficiently handled— but only to a point. For instance, a violinist with a pain in his arm goes to the doctor. Most thinking people do adopt the technological approach to suffering as their first resort. As William Barrett indicates in *The Left Hand of God,* in case of sickness, two boys are sent for the doctor, one for the priest—a conservative estimate of technology's Hooper rating in our culture today. Now, the doctor treats the violinist's arm as a problem. He spots arthritis, and immediately takes steps to eradicate the factor which is most transparent to his medical technique.

What happens, however, when the patient out of the deep chagrin of his thwarted spirit, mutters in the doctor's presence, "Doctor, what is pain?" If the doctor is living as a man, he should be staggered by the question. He should be reduced to reverent taciturnity. If he tries to answer *as a Doctor,* he is a quack. A quack is one who, by definition, misapplies an otherwise legitimate method. When the technologist reaches into his bag of tools for an

instrument by which to expose a mystery, he is on the
verge of malpractice. The question of the meaning of pain
is one such mystery. The answer to it is not entirely before
us.

But Doctors of Philosophy—metaphysicians, so to speak
—are in the same peril of malpractice as Doctors of Medicine. For no one is so accustomed to approaching the
mystery of pain as if it were a problem as are philosophers
themselves. They are almost vocationally predisposed to
give theoretical answers to all questions. To add to their
vulnerability with the crisis of suffering, the whole matter
is generally prejudiced in advance by being classified not
simply as a problem but as a problem of *evil*.

Now as metaphysicians, they introduce the ultimate
dimension by involving God. But the solution, even with
the help of the God-idea, rarely gets beyond the familiar
impasse written up in college texts on philosophy of religion: Either God is good but weak or He is strong but evil.
Two questions are begged by that procedure. In the first
place, suffering has been treated merely as a problem
when actually it is also a mystery. Anything involving God
is a mystery, for to the extent that God is involved, the
situation cannot be entirely open to us. In the second
place, suffering has been maligned as an evil. Inasmuch
as that is really what the question about suffering largely
seeks to determine, it is uninstructively impatient to raise
a question which in the very asking obviates the search for
the answer.

The late Dean of St. Paul's Cathedral, William R. Inge,
did all sufferers a great service. He spent a lifetime in
search of a solution to the "problem of evil." But at the
age of ninety he announced that he had done so without

success. This biographical note will not deter either technologists or metaphysicians from their conscientious approach to this "crisis," and it ought not. But it surely does encourage a shift in the base of operations to non-technological and non-speculative levels of life, levels which admit of mystery and a kind of reality which, though it does not answer to the acquisitive tactics of the rational grasp, does have ways of breaking open its secrets to man and answering his deepest questions.

No great encouragement is given in culture to this shift. For modern life is dominated by technology and its spiritual counterpart, secularism. Secularism rules suffering out as an ultimate possibility. Suffering is an unacceptable condition of things and must be rejected. Ivan in Dostoevsky's *The Brothers Karamazov* speaks for modern man. If God has offered man suffering as a pass through life, he for one must respectfully return the ticket. But Ivan is, as is modern secularism, rebellious. Suffering is received as an attack upon the concept he has of himself as invulnerable. When modern man falls ill, he rebels as children do when thwarted in a determined plan. "Why did this happen to me?" is not for him a question. It is an acrimonious complaint and usually escapes his lips, translated into the language of incredulity: "This can't happen to me!" Outside of the novels of Dostoevsky, probably the most telling exposé of this rejection of the significance of suffering has come from three sources: from Freud, Nietzsche, and Kierkegaard. I do not mean that these modern prophets necessarily attribute any ultimate significance to suffering. I only mean that they deal with the crisis in such a way as to do credit to the dimension of ultimate meaning within it.

According to the psychoanalysis of Freud, much of our suffering is self-inflicted. It is our way of escaping the burden of life. As children, when the going got difficult we could run home to mother. As men, we have the same desires to run, but we express them in socially acceptable forms such as illness. A crippling allergy is much easier to explain to your friends than a failure in business. And if one can manage to let his failure in business be explained by the persistence of the allergy, he has managed very acceptably. One learns to trade major pains for minor, to barter sufferings we ought to bear for those not included in life's original bargain. Suffering can be, as Karen Horney put it, "an opiate against pain," "our recoil from an active mastery of life."

In this sense, the recessive type of personality is the greatest sufferer. The evidence for this phenomenon is obvious: the appearance of disease in some people coincides with the reduction of anxiety. And when the disease is cured, the anxiety has a way of reappearing. One accuses himself with diseases to stave off the accusations of others. You do not hit a man when he is down. One will resort to illness therefore, in order to avoid reproach in the same way in which he will belittle himself to avoid competition with others. Or one may even fall ill as a means of getting one's own way, of soliciting affection and help while at the same time escaping responsibility toward others. He may even choose sickness as a weapon of attack upon others, thinking all the while, "If you hadn't been so mean to me, this never would have happened." The recessive, therefore, often appear as the noblest martyrs in their suffering. They do not ask, "Why did this happen to me?" and they indulgently refuse to allow you to ask it in their presence. The question might unleash a problem which would uncover the real source of the suffering within the soul's desire. How keenly Luther saw to the heart of these demonic possibilities when he said, "The physicians see not that often the devil casts a sickness upon one without any natural causes."

Nietzsche suffered deeply. But he did not deplore his suffering as if it had cancelled out the joy of living. Suffering for him was inseparable from the joy. Not that man enjoys suffering. It is rather that the pursuit of the noblest goals in life seems inextricably bound up with suffering. Both pain and pleasure can be regarded as incidental to the achievements which could be accompanied by either pain or pleasure. "Who ever has a reason for living," Nietzsche said, "endures almost any mode of life." Indeed, if joy itself were carefully examined, it would probably reveal itself to be "a kind of pain," "a rhythm of little stimulations of displeasure." Goethe quite anticipated Nietzsche's mood, then, when he wrote in *Tasso,*

> "Spare not the sick man, dear Physician. Give
> The medicine to him and do not think
> If it be bitter. Whether he recover
> That do consider, good and clever friend!"

Kierkegaard makes an even more positive case for suffering as an ultimately meaningful thing. Unlike the others he seeks support for his view in the Bible. Paul the Apostle has claimed that there is joy in suffering, for "Suffering produces endurance, and endurance produces character, and character produces hope." (Rom. 5:3,4) Or, as Sakini says in his more temperate version in the epilogue of *Teahouse of the August Moon,* "Suffering makes men think, thinking makes them wise, and wisdom makes the world endurable."

Suffering according to Kierkegaard is not simply incidental to a life of great achievement; it is instrumental to it. This is why there can be joy in suffering: you can know that it is not an irritation accidental to the process of life. It *is* the process. "The way of purification is in affliction." It is not the way which is narrow. Narrowness is the way. Hence, the joy in suffering. The joy is in knowing that the way of suffering is the right way.

Kierkegaard would probably support the sentiment in the story of the Greek warrior, Philoctetes, celebrated in Edmund Wilson's *The Wound and the Bow*. Philoctetes is the mythical hero of every sensitive and suffering artist. It is said that he was forced to isolate himself from his community in virtue of the revolting odor of a running sore. Yet his services were constantly demanded by his fellow citizens because of their reliance on the flawless marksmanship of a bow in his possession. By some leap of logic, the presence of pain has been thought by many, including Kierkegaard, to be responsible for the talent of perception in saints and artists. Suffering, it is believed, produces *that* kind of hope. Carried away by the same sentiment, the poet Rilke could say, without resort to Biblical faith,

> "How much there is to suffer! Who would guess
> There'd once been time for laughter and repose?
> And yet I know, better than most of those
> That knew a resurrection, blessedness."

The citation of these instances does not constitute endorsement. They are simply meant as evidence of certain movements of thought in our recent past which take suffering with complete seriousness. They have the merit of resisting the more popular tendency to foreclose the question about suffering, treating it at a simply technological level or dismissing it as an unacceptable evil. The modern man is epitomized by the little girl at a Christmas party. Among the gifts offered her she wanted a doll. But she feared to take it lest she be required to give it away to some relative. So she simply said, "I don't want anything." What she meant was, "I want anything I can have without suffering." Like Dostoevsky's Ivan, she would accept no route through life which came at the price of pain.

This seems, on the surface of it, to violate the spirit in Christianity which, as Kierkegaard saw, rejoices in suffering. A Christian, after all, is one whose strength is made perfect in weakness (II Cor. 12:9,10), who desires to suffer with Christ (Rom. 8:17), as Christ suffered (2 Peter 2:20 ff), on account of the suffering of Christ (Acts 9:16, Phil. 1:29), and even by permission of Christ (Phil. 1:29, 1 Peter 2:20). Hence the Christian life is not a victory over pain, but through pain, which means that suffering cannot be simply classified as an evil: it may be a good. Nor can it be cited as a problem: it may be a third sacrament through which, as Calvin said, Christians are led "by the discipline of the cross into a deeper knowledge of themselves." "I choose everything," said Theresa of Avila. "I will accept everything, the suffering that is inseparable from the joy, and the joy that is the crown of suffering."

The position expressed here might be called a kind of Christian eudaimonism: a theory of blessedness which includes not only the possibility but the necessity of pain to a wholesome, happy life. There is a good deal of common sense in this, so much so that it is not at all unique to Christianity. The sentiment appears widely in the philosophies and religions of the world and in current treatises on meeting pain with bravery. The Arabs have a saying: "All sunshine makes a desert." This is a hard saying during the monsoon. But the point is that visions of drought should make the monsoon endurable. The Buddhists have a story about a young mother who brings the body of her dead baby to the Buddha for miraculous resurrection. The Buddha does not deny the request. He simply requires the woman first to find one family where people live without sorrow. The woman returns from her tour with only one purpose: to withdraw her request. In Wagner's *Tannhauser* a tenor sings a "Hymn to Venus" in which he longs to return to earth where pleasure is mingled with pain. Horace Bushnell in one of his "Sermons on Living Subjects" goes on record in a similar vein: "If the world was a place of good feeling and health and jocund life it would be God's pasture only, not his kingdom." Schleiermacher in a sermon preached after a cholera epidemic says, "If we were left entirely without chastening, of which all the children of God are partakers, we should have no right to consider ourselves sons, but only bastards." John Gunther in *Death Be Not Proud,* the moving story of his son's illness and death, is most convincing. First he cries out to God, "Is there nothing I can do for my boy?" No improvement. He tries again with a new direction, "Is there nothing *You* can do for my boy?" No improvement. And, then, one day the boy sagely suggests to his father, "Maybe *God* is doing something for *you.*" Or, as the young prince said to the spastic boy, "You must be

God's favorite pupil. He gave you the hardest problem."
"The chastisement of our peace," the suffering that "makes
us whole!" (Is. 53:5 R.S.V.)

I, with Ivan, refuse that ticket, but for a different reason.
It is sheer paganism, and what is the same, sheer senti-
mentalized Christianity, sheer Stoicism. The sick man does
not praise the surgeon while he is operating, as the Stoic
Seneca said. But neither does he praise him afterward if
the operation was not "indicated." Must character and the
aesthetic roundness of life be purchased with pain? It is
true that the irritation of a grain of sand provokes the
oyster to produce a pearl. But in all the economy of existence, who needs pearls? I would not say as Ivan does, "All
the knowledge in the world is not worth a child's tears."
I would simply say, the Christian faith does not require
such a deal.

The New Testament would have to be distorted to support the position that suffering and pain are sent by God
as character-builders or as avenues of artistic insight. The
suffering which is in any way endorsed as good is the
suffering that results almost accidentally when Christians
take the stance of discipleship in this God-damning world.
Calvin writes a prescription for suffering which virtually
makes it the medicine of salvation, a third sacrament. But
he is wrong if he means any other suffering than the
suffering which is the by-product of discipleship. He says
that suffering is the sign and seal of our election. "We
are predestined to be conformed to the image of God's
son, and when we suffer, we have the testimony to that
conformity." This statement would make a hypochondriac
of every Presbyterian if the reference to suffering were
stretched to mean more than the sufferings of discipleship.

It is not meant to cover the blind wretchedness forced upon us by an apparently unfeeling universe. A Japanese poet has written a startling quatrain:

> "When I would pray,
> 'Lord, take the thorn away,'
> Clearly there comes to me
> A vision of His cross!"

But I can testify that for me the sentiment is false the moment I learn the poet is a leper.

The a-Christian French mystic, Simone Weil, was a sufferer. She always envied Christ his crucifixion—probably too intensely: she died at age thirty-three. In her *Waiting for God* the following note on suffering appears: "Suffering: the superiority of man over God. We needed the Incarnation to keep that superiority from becoming a scandal!"

What she says is very true. God was in Christ, reconciling the world unto himself at great cost to himself. What she meant is very false, namely, that to suffer is better than not to suffer. The suffering of God in Christ like the suffering of the disciples of Christ is not just indiscriminate wretchedness. It is suffering contracted in the line of holy duty. And it is not just a kind of divine charade in which God dips His finger into this suffering world in order to say, "You see, it hurts me, too." It is the divine revelation to a suffering world that in the world there will always be suffering, even for God. As Dietrich Bonhoeffer recorded in *Prisoner For God,* several days before his genuinely Christian martyrdom in a Nazi concentration camp, "This is the decisive difference between Christianity and all religions. Man's religiosity makes him look

in his distress for the power of God in the world; he uses
God as a *Deus ex machina*. The Bible, however, directs
him to the powerlessness and suffering of God; only a
suffering God can help." The Christian God is one whose
"power is made perfect in weakness." (2 Cor. 12:9)

Now I know why it is that I am so moved by the story
of Felicitas of Carthage, a Christian persecuted in prison
by the pagan Severus. She is an honest Christian who says
"No" to all sentimental efforts to accept suffering as norma-
tive. She will accept it, because she knows God does not
intend it. But she will not confuse it with the radiant
suffering of the martyr who endures pain as a soldier of
Jesus Christ. When she gives birth to her baby there in
prison and when she cries out from the pain, the jailer
half sardonically, half in sympathy asks her, "If you shriek
at that, how do you expect to endure death by beasts?"
And she replies with a canniness that should warrant her
canonization, "Now I suffer what *I* suffer; then another
will be in me who will suffer for me, as I shall suffer for
him."

Suffering incurred through discipleship produces no
crisis. It is the apparently meaningless suffering of everyday life which raises for us the wetched question, "Why
has this happened to me!" All efforts to deal with it are
usually either technological efforts to remove it, specula-
tive efforts to explain it, or sentimental efforts to justify it.
The first does not *attempt* to answer "Why." The second
has never *satisfactorily* answered "Why." The third pur-
veys anesthetic lies about "Why."

Suffering *borne* through discipleship produces no crisis,
either. God can use our evil and meaningless suffering for
good ends, and we can use it as an occasion for disciple-

ship, testifying to God's reality in the patience and radiance with which we bear our meaningless suffering. Aside from that practical solution, however, one lone possibility seems to me to satisfy the concerns and the insights of the Christian faith. Will the mystery break itself open and reveal the intention which lies behind the suffering? If we could know that and if we could justify it, we could accept the suffering without crisis. In the Christian faith that curtain is lifted and this mystery is unveiled: *we can know that God does not intend our suffering.*

At least the doctrine of creation and the doctrine of last things are unanimous in supporting that insight. When God created the world He said that it was good. There is very little in suffering that seems good and very much in suffering that we can get along without. What else explains it? We can only conclude, as the Bible does, that something else has entered between creation and this life of suffering which is evil. Sin does cause suffering. As Luther said, anticipating psychosomatic medicine, suffering is often "a result of sorrow which is often the cause of much disorders; for when the heart is troubled and sorrowful, there follows also weakness of the body. The diseases of the heart are the real diseases." Or as Pascal said, the soul is like the lungs; it has no nerves with which to feel suffering. But the ills of the soul do eventually erupt at a level of experience where we can feel them. "Grant that I may well recognize that the ills of the body are both but the outward image and punishment of the ills of the soul. But, Lord, grant also that they be their cure, by making me behold in the pains which I feel the pain which I did not feel in my soul, though my soul is quite ill and covered with ulcers."

It is difficult to explain on this basis how the vast cosmic evils, such as floods and earthquakes, can be the effects of sin. But it is the Biblical judgment that "the whole creation groaneth and travaileth" not because God wills it so, but because something alien and demonic has entered in to resist his creative purposes.

Even though God does not intend our suffering, as preserver of the universe He supports it. Is that not as bad? Definitely not. Whereas I have not ruled suffering out as a possibility and I have not classified suffering as evil but only as the result of evil, I have refused to attribute it to the intention of God. Even the suffering of Job is a sporting contract which the Devil induced God to allow for only a trial period. The Devil himself carries out the contract. Paul's famous thorn in the flesh has the same sponsorship: "A thorn was given me in the flesh, a messenger of Satan, to harass me." (2 Cor. 12:7) To know that our suffering is not in *God's* purpose—whatever else be true of it—is to give us the spiritual grounds for equanimity in suffering.

Edwin Lewis tutored me in this understanding with great force. Note the position he takes in one of his later volumes, *The Creator and the Adversary*.

"To know, not that God creates the evil but hates it, to know that it rises up against him as it does against us, to know that its conquest is a problem for him as it is for us, to know that it will yield, if it yield at all, not to a gesture of omnipotence but to the steady persistence of suffering love—to know this is not to change anything in the character of the human situation.

"Something, nevertheless, is changed. The *approach* to the situation is changed. There is a change in the *resources* available for meeting it. There is a change in the ultimate *expectation.*" (p. 21)

When I manhandle my young son, I sometimes inflict real pain. Now there are times when I am intending the pain, as in an act of disciplinary punishment. There are other times when we are just sporting around and the pain is utterly incidental to the process. Both forms of pain would weigh the same if judged by the test of pressure. But do they *feel* the same? There lies the key: they do not. And why not? My son is still young enough to cry when hurt. But I have noticed a very revealing practice on his part. When he is hurt at my hand, he will never burst into tears without first consulting my eyes. If he sees there the dark clouds of parental judgment, he will shower forth in corresponding tears. If he sees merriment and approval in my eyes, the pain he surely feels will constitute no crisis for him. James D. Burns' familiar hymn almost says this about our relationship to God through suffering, except for the uncertain fourth line, which I have altered here to suit what I believe is the profounder Christian purpose:

> "Every day will be the brighter
> When Thy gracious face we see;
> Every burden will be lighter
> When we know *what* comes from Thee."

A young mother of an eight-year-old boy lost her husband from a cruel disease. Fairly tearing at me through her sobs, she cried, "For eight years I've taught my boy that God is love! Now what shall I tell him?" The time of bereavement is not the time for sober theology. But I could only feel it was a pity that this mother thought now was the time to relinquish the very affirmation which was designed for just such a time. God *is* love! How else explain the victory of Job over his putrescent, suppurating wounds? He had consulted the eyes of God and did not see God's intention in his suffering. How else explain the radiance of John of the Cross in a suffering so resolute, so uncomplaining, so sporting that it was said of him, unlike Philoctetes, that the pus from his sores gave out a sweet odor like flowers.

Everything that is claimed in the Christian doctrine of creation is reaffirmed in the doctrine of last things. You would expect that, knowing who God is, the Being who is "from everlasting to everlasting," and that His revelation in Jesus Christ is both "the beginning and the end." The doctrine of last things reaffirms that the suffering of man is not in the intention of God. Life will ultimately be conformed without resistance to the divine intent. "We shall all be changed." There shall be "no more tears." The hope of the last things is not something for which we must await the passage of time or transfiguration to a heavenly realm. That form of understanding could reduce the will to live, a piece of bad therapy which every doctor fears in Christian people who look for happiness not *in* but *beyond* this world. The knowledge that God does not intend our suffering minimizes the agony of this present age to the status of a pregnancy. Its days are numbered. "Our affliction is but for a moment." (2 Cor. 4:17) It will not last forever. And you can stand almost anything if you know that it is not going to last forever.

This is one thing John Donne never really saw, and to his hurt. He had no joy in suffering, for he had not resolved the issue as to what God intended in suffering. He said, "Whether thy mercy or thy correction were thy primary and original intention in this sickness I cannot conclude, though death conclude me."

No man needs to live in the torture of that uncertainty. God has revealed in Christ the secret of His purpose for creation. It is a covenant of love with mankind. And God has purposed through His son to establish at the end what He had planned at the beginning, namely, a world that is good. A man can see himself in the mirror of God's Son. And when he does all counterfeit will be removed. The means for a negotiable life will be at hand. Understood in that light, this stanza from James D. Burns' hymn can stand unaltered:

> "Spread thy love's broad banner o'er us;
> Give us strength to serve and wait
> Till thy glory breaks before us
> Through the city's open gate."

EIGHT

The Crisis of Death

"Death is easier to bear when one does not think of it than the thought of death when one is not in danger."

—BLAISE PASCAL, *Pensées.*

"The man who perceives and comprehends his unique situation is distinguished from those who do not in that he always realizes he will die and never need fear in the presence of death. One must even say: as far as Christian theology is concerned, that is the central, the decisive criterion."

—KARL BARTH, *Die Kirchliche Dogmatik* III, 4.

Every man really faces two deaths and not just one. There is the biological event marked by mortuaries and monuments. But there is also the personal event, the spiritual death which often goes unnoticed. The spiritual death, however, is the death which is the greater crisis. It is what the Book of Revelation calls "the second death." The first death, the biological death, no one can escape. That death is written into the structure of things and falls alike upon the just and the unjust. But the second death is avoidable, requiring a decision just as any question of meaning or attitude does. The first death is necessary, but it is not necessary to "be hurt by the second death." (Rev. 2:11) As Kierkegaard put it, "There are many other decisions in life, but only one is decisive in the manner of death."

"As soon as a man is born he is old enough to die." An

old German proverb says that and it is true. But it is only partially true, for the more critical facts about life hold that even though a man may be alive, he can in some sense be dead already. The seer of the Book of Revelation saw through to this layer of death beneath all visible life when he said of the Church at Sardis, "I know your works; you have the name of being alive and you are dead." (3:1) So did the poet Rilke, when he said the deadliest death of all is to be alive and not to know it; and Kierkegaard, who said the real death is not to be able to die.

The second death is the personal event which sets in long before the natural event. A man is a being who *knows* he dies. He attaches *meaning* to his death. The death itself is quite natural and benevolent, like the rain on the just and the unjust. Apart from biological death the universe would be quite uninhabitable, spatially. But because men know and attach meaning to their death, they suffer a possible second death in death. That is the real crisis which may make their lives psychologically uninhabitable. One may die as trees go down in forests, with no sense of meaning because there is no one to observe it. In that case death has decorum but it has no dignity, as William Faulkner once remarked. The second death, which is the natural death as observed through personal concern, may have no decorum. It may be petulant and restive. It may be irresolute and rebellious. But it does have dignity. It has the dignity which one attaches to all characteristically human enterprises where one faces squarely the matter of his ultimate destiny and throws the weight of his decision to one side or another.

According to the New Testament a man can simply die, or he can die in Christ. But if one dies in Christ, he has already conquered the second death, even though the natural culmination of his life still lies ahead. (Rom. 6:11; 1 Thess. 4:16; 1 Cor. 15:18) Death for the Bible is not simply the last moment of life; it is the last enemy. Because of that it is not something to be endured at the end of life but something to be conquered within life itself. One can say, then, of death what the Roman Catholic says of sin: there is a venial death and there is a mortal death. Life in Christ makes death utterly venial, that is, harmless, for while it does nothing to avert the natural death, it already conquers the second death, introducing freedom from the fear of death. To live in Christ is to have eternal life already in this life, so that in spite of man's biological end, death has lost its power over man.

The distinctively human elements in death point to the problem of the second death. That is why it is humane and humanistic of the Bible to "teach us to number our days." (Ps. 90:12; 37:5) For without the continual reminder that he is a being who is living toward death, man could die neglecting to apply "his heart unto wisdom." In that case, his death would be a double death, a *mortal* death. Voltaire has said, "A child brought up alone and transported to a desert island would have no more idea of death than a cat or a plant." Now at first glance it might seem a malediction to remind a child that some day he must die. But is not that very instruction a valediction from vegetative and animal levels of life into mature humanity where one grapples in concern over the meaning and destiny of life? How many funeral parlor advertisements placed in the pews of churches have fanned men into maturity with the sheer reminder that some day a man must die. All men *will* die. That is a biological certainty. But do not all men have a right to a death of their own, to a private death, to what Rilke called "a proper death"?

Gabriel Marcel has commented on his responsibilities during the first world war. He had two functions connected with fatalities in battle. The first was simply to compile the statistics. The second was to send the telegram of announcement to the next of kin. One cannot engage in this dichotomous handling of death without feeling through his own being death's double character. No one would consent to exhausting the significance of death in the category of statistics. It is the second death, the possibility inherent in the *meaning* of death to life, which concerns the next of kin. Martin Heidegger is therefore right and wise to point out that Christian theology from Paul to Calvin has been written in the *consciousness* of death. For the unsuppressed knowledge about death unveils the deepest and most crucial possibilities in life. Philip of Macedon turned this realization into a kind of one-a-day brand elixir. His slave had a standing order. Every morning he was to enter the quarters of his king and shout, "Philip, remember that thou must die!"

Now what could be achieved by that announcement except sharp panic contractions at the breast? "Death is easier to bear," as Pascal has said, "when one does not think of it than the thought of death when one is not in danger." So why think about it? Why keep all life under fear by the *memento mori* when one might just as well screen off that fear through forgetfulness? Why think about what only evokes unpleasant states? Why *precipitate* crises?

The answer is that life is already a second death unless

the fact of death has been confronted and the incipient
fears overcome. The fear of death is itself the second death.
Its force is so efficient that it recapitulates all the basic fears
which make of life a crisis. If it is true, as Luther says in
his *Commentary on Galatians,* that "the fear of death is
thereby death itself"; and if it is true that "he who abolishes
that fear from the heart neither tastes nor feels death";
then this is something about which a person has a right to
know during life.

In the fourteenth century the artist Holbein did a series
of woodcuts called "The Dance of Death." Every station in
life was shown: from king to peasant, cardinal to priest,
grandparent to infant. Insinuated somewhere into each
picture was death in all its skeletal starkness. "Death is no
respecter of persons," these pictures seem to say. "Therefore, King Philip, remember that *thou* must die!"

My purpose here will be similar to Holbein's, with one
exception. I will attempt to show not merely how death
is imminent to all the stations in life but how the second
death, the fear of death invades and recapitulates all our
basic crises.

1. Death and Suffering

Death comes as a reprieve to those whose suffering is
intolerable. Therefore, one should be very careful to
indicate that these influential lines from Baudelaire appear
in a poem entitled "The Death of the *Poor*":

> "Death is our one comfort. . . .
> The very goal of life."

An untimely death, however, is one of the gravest occa-
sions for suffering, inducing an acute sense of pique. Take,

for instance, the dramatic case of Paul-Louis Landsberg, promising young German philosopher, hunted down by Nazism. Just before dying of exhaustion in a concentration camp at age forty-two, he wrote, "To imagine a vital suffering, however atrocious the suffering may be, has in it something even relatively consoling. . . . Life is our country, even when it is pain and compassion. . . . Confronted by actual death, however, we seem banished from our own world."

The artist Raphael died at age thirty-six. Some defended the universe by saying life is a quality: Raphael had achieved it sooner than others. Nietzsche rightly lashed out against this pious apology. "It is only because you do not know what a *natura naturans* like Raphael is, that you are not on fire when you think it existed once and can never exist again."

The consolations of theology are the same for death as for suffering. God does not intend an untimely death. It is wrong-headed to say that God wills any man's death. Death as the crown of life, yes: when all possibilities have been fulfilled and death emerges as the ripeness implicit in life itself. In that sense it is true, as the dialogues of Job reveal, that the Lord giveth and the Lord taketh away—"blessed be the name of the Lord." But death as the Satanic prankster who poisons the brew of life before the thirst is quenched—that death should not be coddled theologically.

"Why does God *permit* it?" I do not believe that an honest theology can answer that question except to say that God does not *intend* it. But that answer will not satisfy those who have an abstract, non-Biblical concept of God's omnipotence, as if God should be able immediately to back up all His intentions with force. And it will seem like hedging to those who are willing to exploit the lamb-like meekness of pious people who capitulate unquestioningly to everything in life as though it were sent from God. To say that it is God's will that a man die an untimely death may be an opiate for those susceptible to such drugs. However, theology is in the service not of deliverance from momentary pain, but of the truth about our life with God. The Biblical position can allow that God is the creator of death as a natural event. But an untimely death is a form of suffering which has intervened between the creator and the universe He sustains. During the age of this world, which is the age not of God's creation but only of His preservation, it is *in Adam* and not simply in God that all men live; and it is in Adam that all men die. A strong case could be made to the effect that while death is implicit in creation, the untimely death is the invention of the devil and at his disposal in this age of Adam. (cf. Hebrews 2:14)

To know that God does not intend this untimely banishment from our own world is enough to quiet the panic which honest men have about the suffering of death. But to know further that God has provided another country beyond this world as a continued habitation, and that those who die will be resurrected from the dead, is the full truth about God's power over death. The Christian faith does not give us detailed descriptions about the life after death. The New Testament is candidly silent about the conditions that will obtain following our exile from this world. But it is unequivocal about the truth which is of major importance: the God who does not intend our untimely death will have the last word about death. That

word will be the word of resurrection which creates our
life anew and with it the possibilities of the ripening of
our years under conditions vastly more favorable to
fruition than those that here prevail.

To suffer pique about death is itself a form of
the second death. The sarcasm and defiance in the voice of
the poet Dylan Thomas is magnificent as he reads his lines
on "A Refusal to Mourn the Death, by Fire, of a Child
in London." (Caedman Recording TC 1018) It is Christian. It is mankind's brave "No" to Satan who has the
power of death. By itself, however, it is as wrong as all
part truths. When applied to the crisis of death, it is a
poisonous wrong, a devil's brew accelerating the very
process of death. The poet's bilious attitude toward life
may have contributed to his own untimely death. How
incomplete, how self-deceptive, then, is the concluding
line of this same poem.

"After the first death there is no other."

An acrimonious attitude toward the first death is already
creating the second death. It makes of death a crisis. From
this second death trust in the God who raises from the
dead can deliver us. For this purpose Jesus Christ took
death upon himself, "that through death he might destroy
him who has the power of death, that is, the devil, and
deliver all those who through fear of death were subject
to lifelong bondage." (Heb. 2:14,15)

2. Death and Marriage

Death does to marriage what God allows no man to do.
It puts asunder. When that happens, grief is imminent as
a painful crisis. Marriage makes of a man and a woman

one flesh. Death tears that flesh in two and, through the loss of one to death, leaves the other a mere remnant of a person. That experience of fragmentariness is known to us as grief.

Not all grief is a *bona fide* confrontation with death. Much of the most acute expression of grief is really a manifestation of anxieties. Death only provides an occasion for their expression. Anxious expressions of grief run the whole emotional gamut from acute shock to sheer imperturbability. And in between is a disturbing experience, which one dare not even admit to himself, of actual gratification at another's death.

The rebellious type personality can be either gravely shocked or secretly gratified by the event of a death. He is shocked, of course, because death constitutes a loss, and he holds the concept of himself as one who never loses. But death is the gambler that wins in every toss. Under other circumstances, death may please the rebellious, if by the event some threat to one's own supremacy is warded off.

The recessive type is also shocked by death, but for a different reason. The death of another exteriorizes his own fear of inadequacy about life. "No man is an island," he says, when he hears the bell toll. But it is not clear whether he feels diminished by the death of another, as Donne implies, or threatened: "Send not to hear for whom the bell tolls. It tolls *for thee*." Just as often, however, the recessive will feel some tickle in his groin over another's death. For one thing, bereavement supports his sense of need for self-accusation and punishment. For another, the basis that bereavement gives for the sympathetic attention of others nourishes one's hunger for approval. Hence, the recessive can be detected among those who protract the mourning period to unreasonable lengths.

The subterfuge employed in these morbid exploitations of grief may suggest an even deeper problem, the problem of guilt. Joshua Liebman's classic *Peace of Mind* makes it quite clear that the woman who weeps interminably at the death of her husband need not be weeping out of grief. It is not necessarily that she is so sorry he is dead. It may as well be that she is so sorry she is so glad he is dead!

The resigned type has no reaction to death. He is unmoved. Being completely detached from others, he finds the loss of them no loss to him. Witness the conversation which I overheard between two Manhattan cab drivers, shouting out of their windows while weaving down Fifth Avenue:

"Heard about Joe?"

"Yeah!"

"Too bad, eh?"

"How old was he?"

"Fifty-two!"

"Oh well, when your time's up, y'gotta go!"

The theology of grief is a heartless thing. But then theology is useless under conditions of stress. The time for a reflective faith is before the need grows critical. A life well enforced by adequately Christian understandings of life can avert or at least weather the critical situations. Why, for instance, should it not be known from the beginning that all men are mortal, that all flesh is grass which withereth, and that all life must be held with the same tentativeness with which one holds something so transitory as a hillside daisy?

There is no more moving and reliable theology of grief

to be found than in the *Confessions* of Saint Augustine, who knew about grief at first hand from the loss of his best friend and of his mother, Monica. According to Augustine, people undergo acute grief generally for two reasons. On the one hand, they love others as if they would never die. They should love men as men, that is, as mortals. Then they would never be shocked grievously when mortality takes its claim. For another thing, they look upon death as a loss and grieve their losses. They hold to the lives of others as if they possessed those lives, whereas only God really possesses the lives of others, hence only God has a right to grieve, because only God legitimately can lose. Marriage, in which loss by death is usually the most traumatic, is the area in which this truth should be the most apparent. It is the essence of marriage that two become one, hence to be rent apart by death is serious. But it is also the essence of marriage that each *give* himself to the other while receiving the other with no sense of possessiveness. Berdyaev's advice to "treat the living as though they were dying" may not make for the merriest marriage. But realistically, King Philip's wife needs to hear as often as the king himself, "Remember, King Philip must some day die." Death will necessarily disrupt all marriage. But the second death which is the crisis of grief can be averted if one is willing to surrender what was intended originally only as a gift.

3. Death and Vocation

When death sidles up to a man at his work it wears the most sinister grin of all. For to rob a man of the chance to fulfill his vocation is to rob him of his self-vindication. The author whose manuscript is unintelligibly incomplete, the artist whose canvas is just beginning to round itself out, the athlete who has just caught his stride! When death taps these it is a swindle and a cheat. Sensing this problem, Max Scheler makes the realization of death an attribute of the experience of growing old. The closer one gets to the deadline of his life, the more acute is his sense of the loss of this freedom to make something out of his life. But those who engage with Philip of Macedon, as I suggest they should, in the *memento mori,* court some very distasteful by-products of the awareness of death. They run the risk of engaging in what Dietrich Bonhoeffer has called "the idolization of death." I gather he means they take death so seriously that they are forced into some untenable attitudes toward life. They teeter in an unhappy balance between two equally disastrous pits. One may "cling convulsively" to life out of his sense of the imminence of death. Another may simply cast life away. In either case, the sense of death will have a profound effect upon one's conduct of life, which is probably why Karl Barth has chosen to deal extensively with the problem of death in the ethics section of his systematic theology.

Take for instance the case of the young German soldier facing almost certain death in the battle for Stalingrad. In his last letter home he writes, "I have no fear, but my heart is sad. . . . A hollow indifference has seized me and cripples every activity. . . . It does not pay to fight and die for this shadow world." There is a recessive mechanism in this reaction to the threat of death. Seeing the dwindling possibility of vindicating one's existence in life, one chooses the extreme of virtual inactivity. Cheated and discouraged, he surrenders himself to the altar of death, and in the very act, brands life as meaningless.

On the other hand, a rebellious possibility is present. The threat of death may rather elicit from a man what Calvin calls "the diabolical furor of immortal fame." Men cling to life just that convulsively for fear that death will intervene too soon and cheat them of their rightful consummation. Dostoevsky has written of this passion in his novel, *The Idiot*. He tells of a young man recounting his experience of living under the sentence of death. "He said that nothing was so dreadful at that time as the continual thought, 'What if I were not to die! What if I could go back to life—what eternity! And it would be all mine! I would turn every minute into an age; I would lose nothing. I would count every minute as it passed, I would not waste one!' He said that this idea turned to such a fury at last that he longed to be shot quickly."

There develops from this a very important insight about the Christian faith. It is the widespread custom of believing that the Christian's hope in the eternal life undercuts the seriousness with which he holds this present life. It would seem that just the opposite is true. Those who take death too seriously are the ones who either take life too lightly or take life too seriously. If death is the last word, then either one must despair of living or he must live as if this life were his eternity. But if he knows—as Albert Schweitzer suggests Paul the Apostle did—if he knows that this world is "a house sold for the breaking up," he will live in it with care; but he will not invest his entire holdings in it. Or, as Dietrich Bonhoeffer says in his *Ethics,* quite reasonably and quite Biblically, "Wherever it is recognized that the power of death has been broken, wherever the world of death is illumined by the miracle of the resurrection and of the new life, . . . one neither clings convulsively to life nor casts it away."

The second death is the sense of being cheated. It can turn life into a fevered race with death, or it can cut the nerve of life and make it limp. The gospel of the resurrection refuses to concede finality to death, and in the process comes as a respite in life from the less tolerable pressures of so ultimate a deadline. "In the Lord your labor is not in vain" for in him "Death is swallowed up in victory." (1 Cor. 15:54-58)

4. Death and Doubt

Death precipitates a very interesting professional crisis. Who of all the professional people can help a man through death? The medic, of course, can help him before death, but that is finally too little. The mortician can help him after death, but that is always too late. Who is there to administer the salve which can reduce the sting of death itself? The mortician can rouge the face of death and make it seem to the living not quite so ghastly. The medic can anesthetize the last painful gasps of the dying and thus quite bountifully reduce its wretchedness. But who can grapple with the fact of death itself? I say, with every expectation of being charged with professional pride, that there is only one—the minister. He alone has what the Bible calls "the words of eternal life," which is what, at last, the dying man needs.

Now death is a curious kind of doubt-producing situation. For if death has the last word, as it seems, then none of the words spoken on this side of death have any really ultimate meaning. The grin of death laughs them out of existence. Ideas are all finite and death is the last limit of all our knowledges. Only little clusters of meaning can be salvaged from the transitory moments of life. If death has the last word, there is no really ultimate meaning in life. Doubt, then, takes its place alongside death as the reaper. Cutting down the hopes of meaning in life, it is only the foretaste of what death will do in the end.

When the minister speaks about the life beyond death and about the word of meaning which survives the limits of death, it is not strange that he should be doubted. Everything dies including the words by which we strive to salvage deathless meanings. Eternal life, like every profound belief, is a promise, not a certified and demonstrated fact. And like a promise, it can be doubted. But would it not be the final irony of life if one were to entomb as finite the very words which hold out the hope of a meaning which does not die? When the minister, or anyone who witnesses to "the way, the truth, and the life" speaks, he does so in the wheezing vocables which live as all things on this side of death, for but a moment. But he also believes he speaks, so to say, binaurally. Insinuated into his earth-bound speech is a language from another dimension of reality where nothing dies forever. The frequency of its tones is probably too high to be detected in a life with low fidelity. But that tone when it is heard has the capacity to guide a man through death without the threat of meaninglessness, because it comes to him as a signal from beyond this life, as a beacon of permanence in a universe where all things otherwise perish. One crisis of death is this second death of meaninglessness. It is overcome in "the word of life." "Truly, truly, I say to you, he who hears my word and believes him who sent me," said our Lord, "*has* eternal life; he does not come into judgment, but has passed from death to life." (John 5:24) "Heaven and earth will pass away," He said, "but my words will not pass away." (Matt. 24:35)

5. *Death and Guilt*

Death convincingly settles at least one major problem in the world. It kills the possibility of sin. But what it does not kill is the possibility of guilt and its judgment. The sting of death is precisely there. (1 Cor. 15:56) The human imagination with its sense of stern justice visualizes death as the ante-chamber to the supreme tribunal. The courts of heaven are equipped with the most delicate scales and the most exhaustive records of human merits and offenses. The threat of the meaninglessness of life which doubt poses is feeble compared to the threat of condemnation which the conscience of man imagines to lie beyond the grave. A man would rather keep the ills he has than flee to others that he knows not of. As Karl Barth has said, "We have not death to fear, but God."

What can one say to the stricken mourner who cries across the dead body of a loved one, half defiantly half in hope, "Will he be saved?" Will one excuse himself briefly while he computes from memory the virtues and vices of the dead? Or what can one say to a man who, clinging to the thin ledge of life left to him, seeks some assurance about the life beyond, and asks, "Will I be saved?" Will one request a short autobiographical sketch, tallying the score in parallel columns, then give his verdict? I obviously caricature. But I will warrant that more wounds are raw from the fugitive second of uncertainty in response to these questions than are healed by our voluminous responses under more vigilant circumstances.

"Prepare to meet thy God!" That is the answer to every question from the guilt-confessing throat of man. It is about God that the Christian knows best. The Christian knows about man, to be sure. But what he knows about man he has learned from what he knows about God. He knows that man is a being who is responsible for imaging the existence of God in the world. What man is and will be depends entirely upon who God is. And when it comes to the crisis of guilt in death, what does one man know about another? God alone, who seeth in secret, knows the heart of man; and God alone can judge without being judged.

Who, then, is this God whom we prepare in life to meet in death? He is not the God who is the creature of our guilty imagination. He is the God who is the subject of Christ's revelation. He is the God who showed Himself in life as one who did not will the death of any man, who sent His son not to condemn the world but that the world through Him might be saved. He is the God alongside whom His son will sit in the last judgment, to remind Him of His covenant of mercy with mankind. When one dies, *this* is the God he must prepare to meet.

During the first world war Peter T. Forsyth, a Congregational theologian in England, wrote a book designed to console the parents of boys who had died in battle. In it he reduces parental grounds for worry about the destiny of their sons in death. After all, in the eleventh hour of life, under heat of battle, who knows what penitence may not have been evoked by which to pave the way to an eternal life. Is *that* the message for those who are facing the second death of guilt?

A Catholic priest once comforted the widow of a suicide.

Now suicide is a mortal sin, which means the act can only merit mortal death, the second death. But the priest left one opening in the otherwise tight-fitting scheme of things. The man had jumped from a bridge—a *high* bridge. Surely on the way down he had sufficient opportunity for repentance! Is *that* the consolation held out by the gospel?

Karl Stern tells the story of a priest of the eighteenth century who was recommended for canonization. This priest had been at one time a prison chaplain. A stubbornly impenitent criminal resisted every invitation to penitence right to the last. Frustrated finally by the condemned man on the gallows, the priest cried out in the presence of the spectators: "This must be a remarkable moment for all of you—because it is perhaps the only time in your life that you will see a man of whom you can be certain that he will go to hell." It is to the credit of the Church of Rome, which professes an exceeding knowledge of the mechanisms of justice in the after-life, that this priest was refused canonization on the basis of that remark.

Fortunately for us, what we know about the God whom man will meet in death coincides with what we know of hope for man in the life beyond the grave. For we know that man's hope for the future is not conditioned on his past and present but on the disposition and judgment of God. That makes all calculations about man's relative virtue absolutely superfluous. And what *is* the judgment of God? How can we *know* what that will be? We have a reliable clue already. For God has already judged the world in Christ, and He has said yes. He has stated His purpose as reconciliation and not condemnation. He has shown Himself to be a God of mercy. "For our sake he made him to be sin who knew no sin, so that in him we might become the righteousness of God." (2 Cor. 5:21) This knowledge is enough to pull the sting of death and liberate us from that second death of guilt. "Just as it is appointed for men to die once, and after that comes judgment, so Christ, having been offered once to bear the sins of many, will appear a second time, not to deal with sin but to save those who are eagerly waiting for him." (Hebrews 9:27-8)

6. Death and Anxiety

Karl Jaspers has commented in his *Philosophie* that "all anxiety is at base anxiety over death." There is a very good reason for that. The consciousness of death arouses the most acute sense of self-awareness, inspiring the desires and hopes of the human personality. At the same time, the fact of death stands over against all these desires as an inescapable limit, effecting frustration and fear.

No man can take another's place in death. No man can die your death for you any more than he can take your bath for you. This knowledge of one's irreplaceability heightens his self-consciousness. Picture, for instance, as Helmut Thielicke does in *Tod und Leben,* a man walking his dog along the road by the village cemetery. If one could frame the relative mental processes of dog and man at that moment, one could know what it is that distinguishes an animal from a human being. Dogs die *en masse*. Men do, too, so far as their biological death is concerned. But men face the *second* death, which is the anxiety over their death. This is their uniqueness as men, to have a death of their own.

In the Swedish film, "She Danced Only One Summer," two young lovers are pictured in a meadow crowded with daisies. He picks one and hands it to her. She says, "Isn't it a pity that this flower will never live again." He says, "But why! There are thousands of them! And others will grow up in their places next spring!" She says, "But *this* one will never live again."

So man lives his life, facing death in fears arising from a sense of one's utter uniqueness and irreplaceability. Holbein's "Dance of Death" pictured death invading all the stations of life, the great leveller in whose presence all men are the same. It was intended in part as a social document to inspire the overthrow of inequality. The H-bomb in its inartistic way may be producing the same effect upon our time. As some contemporary Holbein in rogue's clothing has said, "This is the age of the H-bomb in which all men are cremated equal." There is a much more poignant by-product to the sense of the universality of death, however. It inspires the sense of the utter uniqueness of each man's life. In the presence of death each man is different. Hence, it contributes to the widespread anxiety over life which everywhere accompanies individualism. "*This one* will never live again."

The sheer physiological realism of naturalistic philosophies has intensified that anxiety in modern times. It has made it increasingly difficult for well-wishers to hold sentimental views about the imperishability of the soul. Inasmuch as there are no instances of souls existing independently of nervous systems, it is difficult to view the inert remains of a corpse and conclude anything else than simply, "He is dead!" Idealisms of one sort and another can protest that nothing so fine as the human mind can be allowed to perish. But naturalism simply says, when the body dies the man dies.

Refreshingly enough, Christianity is on the side of naturalism in this debate. It does not hold out the hope of the immortality of the soul. All flesh is grass, it withereth. When a man dies, he dies completely. Only God is immortal. (John 5:26) We carry the sentence of death within us, as Paul the Apostle said, in order not to trust in ourselves. (2 Cor. 1:9) The Bible knows nothing of the existence of souls independent of bodies. But it does know of the death of bodies, and with them of the very self. Here the philosophical materialist of the seventeenth century, Thomas Hobbes, is on more solid exegetical ground than many Christians when he says, "That the soul of man is in its own nature eternal, and a living creature independent on the body, or than any mere man is immortal otherwise than by the resurrection in the last days, except Enoch and Elias, is a doctrine not apparent in Scripture." (*Leviathan*, Ch. 38)

Indeed, what the Bible professes is not the immortality of the soul but the resurrection of the dead. A man dies completely. If he lives again, it is through the same power that brought him to life in the beginning. The sign of the Christian's hope of resurrection is the resurrection of Jesus Christ from the dead. Because he lives, we shall live. Our future life is contingent not upon some spark of life within us which death never extinguishes. It is contingent upon the resurrection of our Lord who, in conquering sin in the world has thereby conquered death. If there is an immortality, it is not the immortality of the soul but "the immortality of the God relation." (Paul Althaus) The continuity of our life resides not in us but in Him who by His grace has given us the promise of life in Jesus Christ.

In one stroke, then, the Christian faith both confirms and vitiates our anxiety over death. It confirms our individuality, for each man has a death of his own. In a sense, however, it denies the irreplaceability of our death. Each man's death *can* be substituted for—by the death of Jesus Christ. Because he died and rose from the dead, no man needs to die the second death. When we die, we die fully. When we rise, it will be because he died and rose. (2 Cor. 5:14; 2 Tim. 1:10; Romans 8:1-10; Galatians 3) Hence, we can die our death and live it, too. We can have a unique and proper death and still retain the hope of a unique and self-identical life beyond death. We can have the exhilarating anxiety that comes from knowing that each man dies for himself; but we can be delivered from the second death of anxiety. We can know that *"this one"* can live again.

The Christian doctrine of the resurrection is not a cosmographic fantasy about the detailed conditions of an after life. It is the significant assurance that death does not put an end to the possibility of life. A man's life is on the pattern of the Broadway player whose role calls for his death in the first act. The curtain falls. His part is finished. All men are actors who seem fated to die before the play is finished.

As soon as the curtain falls, however, this actor leaps to his feet and dashes across the street to another theatre where he takes up another part. So man dies: to rise. Man's destiny is not explained by one stage only. The doctrine of the resurrection has nothing to do with the nature of the transition one makes from one theatre to another—how long it takes, or his condition on the way. Nor has it to do with the character of the scenery in the new theatre. The hope of resurrection simply inspires the confidence in this stage of life that death is not the end. We may play out our lives upon another stage.

INDEX OF NAMES

INDEX OF SUBJECTS